IN THE MURMURS OF THE ROTTEN CARCASS ECONOMY

IN THE MURMURS OF THE ROTTEN CARCASS ECONOMY

DANIEL BORZUTZKY

NIGHTBOAT BOOKS

NEW YORK

Design and typesetting by HR Hegnauer

Text set in Perpetua and Impact

Cover photograph by Valerie Mejer, *Archivo/Archive*, courtesy of the artist

Cataloging-in-publication data is available from the Library of Congress

Distributed by University Press of New England
One Court Street
Lebanon, NH 03766
www.upne.com

Nightboat Books
New York
www.nightboat.org

This town is filled with echoes. It's like they were trapped behind the walls, or beneath the cobblestones. When you walk you feel like someone's behind you, stepping in your footsteps. You hear rustlings. And people laughing. Laughter that sounds used up. And voices worn away by the years. Sounds like that. But I think the day will come when those sounds fade away.

Juan Rulfo, Pedro Páramo (translated by Margaret Sayers Peden)

It would have been an absence-word, a hole-word, whose center would have been hollowed out into a hole, the kind of hole in which all other words would have been buried. It would have been impossible to utter it, but it would have been made to reverberate. Enormous, endless, an empty gong, it would have held back anyone who had wanted to leave, it would have convinced them of the impossible, it would have made them deaf to any other word save that one, in one fell swoop it would have defined the future and the moment themselves. By its absence, this word ruins all the others, it contaminates them, it is also the dead dog on the beach at high noon, this hole of flesh.

Marguerite Duras, The Ravishing of Lol Stein (translated by Richard Seaver)

MI DIOS ES HAMBRE
Raúl Zurita

Do you want to know what my teacher's name is? It's sand.
Lorenzo Borzutzky, September 1, 2010

*The Bolivians are working with gravity, that's a secret so as not to spread
alarm. But we're getting further with noise and there's thousands dead
of light in Madagascar. Who's going to mobilise darkness and silence?
That's what I wondered in the night.*
Caryl Churchill, Far Away

WRITING

1

"If there weren't things like this," writes Marguerite Duras in 'The Death of the Young British Pilot,' "writing would never take place. But even if writing is there, always ready to scream, to cry, one does not write it. Emotions of that order, very subtle, very profound, very carnal, and essential, and completely unpredictable, can hatch entire lives in a body. That's what writing is. It's the pace of the written word passing through your body. Crossing it. That's where one starts to talk about those emotions that are hard to say, that are so foreign, and yet that suddenly grab hold of you."

"If there weren't things like this," writes Duras, and by things she means anonymous bodies that fall out of airplanes.

He was an orphan and had no family and was found dead in a village in France. One of his school teachers would come from England every year to put flowers on his grave.

"He's a corpse, a twenty-year old corpse who will go on to the end of time."

"If there weren't things like this," writes Duras.

A writing of ghostliness, of anonymous corpses, of anonymous love.

A writing of love, anonymity attention

+ + +

This is a story I was once told: a corpse was thrown out of an airplane.

This is a story that consists not of words but of images.

There is a woman in her apartment. We are at the dining room table, drinking tea, looking out at the smog of a grey winter day.

She is telling me about a family member in C---. She is telling me why he went to live in C--. She is telling me about his brother. Young. A radical. Didn't know what he was doing. Was organizing a factory. There was a girlfriend, maybe she was a wife. The police came in. She pretended like she was one of the workers. Maybe. An image of a scarf, a head wrap, a bandana she pulls over her head to fit in with one of the factory workers.

She is telling me about the man's brother. His name was S-. Arrested at the factory. Trying to organize the workers.

He disappeared.

His parents went to A---, his brother to C--. I don't know the sequences here.

The facts might be wrong.

It doesn't really matter.

His parents moved overseas. They got a call one day. They were asked to fly to a mountain village to identify a body that had an identification card with their son's name on it. They flew across the ocean. Found their way to the mountain village to identify the body. It wasn't their son.

I've thought about these words forever.

I've thought about this story forever and I refuse to verify its authenticity, its truthfulness.

Because it's possible that this story, these images, have been at the root of every single word that I write.

+ + +

Los Murmullos (*The* Murmurs). I read that *Los Murmullos* (*The Murmurs*) was going to be the title of Juan Rulfo's novel *Pedro Páramo.*

Both in English and in Spanish, the word "Murmurs" may very well be the most perfect word in the language.

+ + +

Because of one priest's corruption (and another priest's refusal to absolve the corrupt priest) the dead of an entire town are stuck in purgatory. *Pedro Páramo* is, among other things, a story about bureaucracy, about rules, about murmuring ghosts who get stuck in purgatory because of the corrupt behavior of authoritative bodies. Ethical corruption or perhaps divine corruption which in this case leads to bureaucratic corruption. One wonders about the value of these distinctions.

+ + +

I walk around Chicago transposing the ghostly murmurs of the people of Juan Rulfo's Comala, who were destroyed not just by the bureaucracy of the church but also by Pedro Páramo, the {failed} village capitalist, the guy who owned, or pretended to own, the entire town.

I walk around Chicago, drive west on Montrose Avenue past all the boarded up storefronts, and I hear the murmurs of the ghosts of Comala.

Destroyed, broken there, collapsing: obliterated neighborhoods riddled with ghosts.

And I think about the scene when Susana San Juan, Pedro Páramo's lover, is about to die. She is receiving her final communion, and Father Renteria, the corrupt priest, whispers in her ear:

"I swallow foamy saliva. I chew clumps of dirt crawling with worms that knot in my throat and push against the roof of my mouth... My mouth caves in, contorted, lacerated by gnawing, devouring teeth. My nose grows spongy. My eyeballs liquefy. My hair burns in a single bright blaze...."

These words the last she hears in her life.

2

One day, while I am writing this book, I write the following. That is, I have the following dream while typing on the computer.

I am standing by a fence in the desert. The fence separates country A from country B.

There are bodies climbing over the fence. They get to the top and for a moment they hover between country A and country B. Then they hop down to country B and as they drop their faces fall off their bodies.

They hop down from the fence and search in the mud for their faces. But the lips they find are not their lips, the mouths they find are not their mouths, the eyes they find are not their eyes. But they keep these parts all the same and run into the desert past the early Americans who are napping at the border.

+ + +

This book is filled with nightmares. Pages of writing that are not in the book. Pages of writing that created the book but which in fact it cannot contain.

+ + +

Later I am writing and watching myself walking through the desert, searching for a particular hole when a brutal dog attacks me. It attempts to bite off my arm, but the dog's owner is confused by my skin (it changes colors) so he pulls the dog away, spanks it, and proposes certain theories about the need to alter the dog's intrinsic nature.

What leaks out of the dog is a human combination of love, anger and devotion.

What leaks out of the human is a hybrid combination of intellect, desire, and monstrosity.

I remove my arm before the dog can yank it completely from my body, and when I attempt to patch up the leaking blood I suddenly feel the urge to write.

I dip my finger in the blood and start to compose letters on my skin.

But then there is nothing to say.

+ + +

Another day I keep thinking about a body who writes through sand. In fact the body is me but I'd rather just refer to it as "the body."

It writes through sand and when it emerges on the other side of the fence, the side of the fence whose bureaucracy had promised but failed to take care of it, the body asks certain questions to certain people who it knows will not have the answers.

For instance, it asks a young boy to identify the name of a tree with pink leaves that smells like expensive cologne. It is a tree whose name has no

English translation just as there is no way of translating the experience of the bodies who lost their faces when they fell off the fence. They are whipped by bodies who are controlled by bureaucrats on both sides of the line who believe that the same bag of shit on one side of the line smells better than the same bag of shit on the other.

3

Duras:

"Finding yourself in a hole, at the bottom of a hole, in almost total solitude, and discovering that only writing can save you."

Because I am surrounded by people who murmur with no voice.

Because I am surrounded by people who die with no voice.

Because everywhere houses and streets and cities and states and nations collapse with no voice.

And then one day I am listening to Raúl Zurita speak and he is answering a question about why nature, why the rocks, the sea, and the mountains have been so important to him; and he says that the beaches and the mountains and the sea were so much kinder to the bodies that were thrown out of airplanes than the military or the government had been. He does not explain this any further, and no one presses the point. But afterwards I can't help but think, forever, about absorption. About what it means to be absorbed. About how a community, a city, a country, a nation, absorbs, or refuses to absorb, its bodies, its ghosts, its citizens.

+ + +

A writing of absorption. A writing of envelopment. Of dissolution, evaporation.

Because everywhere there are people with no voice who cannot be absorbed.

Because there are things like this, because there are unabsorbed bodies, writing continues to take place.

4

And then there is this scene at the end of Kafka's "The Judgment":

Georg tucking his sick, weak, and seemingly hopeless father into bed. His father has confessed. He will no longer absorb the fictional life that Georg has presented to him. Georg lifts his father up, strips off his clothes, gets his father into bed. His father pulls up the covers, and, according to one translation they are "tucked…more closely around him," while in another they are "unusually high up over his shoulders."

And then: "Am I well covered up? Don't worry, you're well covered up, says the son." At which point the father explodes with rage and accuses the son of living a lie; he confronts the son about his lies, reveals that he (the father) doesn't actually sit in his room reading enormous newspapers (he just holds old ones over his eyes), and sentences his son to death by drowning, to which the son promptly complies by running out of the house and throwing himself off the first bridge he can find.

"Am I well covered up now?"

These words gave life to the book. They created the book long before the book ever began. Decades with these words, this image: the decaying man about to be covered up; the decaying body desperately fighting to reclaim his voice. A reclamation that can only occur if it kills the thing (the child) it creates.

+ + +

These are the images that created this book: the bodies falling out of airplanes; the man who comes every year to place flowers on the grave of the anonymous, dead pilot; the murmuring ghosts of Comala stuck in the bureaucracies of purgatory; the murmuring ghosts of Comala transposed to the rotten carcass economy of Chicago; the father being covered up by the ungrateful son; the blankets pulled over his head; the words "Am I well covered up now?" A refusal to be covered up; a refusal and a subsequent drowning.

+ + +

And then I am in Chicago and I can't sleep for months and I envision a father and son stuck in a dormitory established for the refugees whose houses have been destroyed in our rotten carcass economy. There are soldiers guarding the dormitory, which is in an abandoned health club. And there is a boy wailing with rotten teeth and he is begging for someone to yank his teeth out and eventually a doctor appears and gives him morphine and pulls his front teeth out; this image is confused with the image of the boy being poisoned by another doctor; the father confronts the doctor who poisons while he is sewing up the wounds of an anonymous body beneath him.

And then I hear:

"Look, there are men here who are instructed to abduct, men who are instructed to rape, men who are instructed to steal, men who are instructed to offer false kindnesses, men who are instructed to rip out hair, to burn, to smile, to tie up, to flatter, to stab, to spit and to feed. I am instructed to poison."

And as the bodies in Chicago come and go between the concrete of the dormitory floor and the mud of the next world, they murmur from one voice to another.

Cover me up, say the voices in the mud: Are we well covered up now?

You are well covered up now, you are well covered up now.

But really they are not covered up at all.

Creaking bones, grinding teeth, a failure in the ability of the mud to muffle the voices of the bodies it covers.

And we say to the murmuring bodies: sleep now forever in the thick and unsleeping mucilage.

And they say: what does the air look like, what does the ceiling look like, what does the blood on the hands, on the walls, on the floor look like?

And we say: the countries are covered up now, the rivers are covered up now, the fathers and mothers are covered up now, the doctors and soldiers are covered up now, the borders are covered up now.

And as the voices from the cover up murmur, we wait for the water to push down the walls, to lift up the cots, to make the dormitory sink through the floor or float off into the mud of the groaning, burbling night.

5

Every book has sentences in it the writer hates, that the writer cannot get rid of, that the writer cannot live without. Any writer who cuts out every sentence he hates is a writer not worth reading.

But what's even worse than this are the sentences the writer loves, the sentences the writer needs, the sentences that created the book but which the writer absolutely cannot include.

"Doubt," writes Duras, "equals writing."

To which I would add that I have little interest in writing that doesn't make a mess: of itself, of the world, of its own reason for being.

One can write towards a reduction. One can begin with a mess of words, and then hope, in the end, for a beautiful and satisfying reduction of that mess. One can consciously work towards a reduction in the ability of the writing body to be absorbed by the words it murmurs to everyone and no one in particular.

+ + +

One day I wrote: "all the bodies in the dormitory, all the bodies in the cots, on the floors, in the stalls, in the closets and lockers, in the pools and showers: they are waiting to know what will happen to them, who will take them, where they will be taken to, how they will get there and what they will do when we get there."

I couldn't keep these words. I had no use for them, even though, inexplicably, they meant everything to me. I couldn't keep these lives. Just as I couldn't keep the water that overtook the streets. And I couldn't keep the looters and thieves and killers that followed the water. And I couldn't keep the journalists who followed the looters and I couldn't keep the soldiers who came to clear away the water and the corpses and the looters.

But I could keep this one voice (it's impossible to explain why). It spoke to me often while I was writing this book. One day, it told me a story. It whispered:

"I remember the day they brought me here. I found a cot and attempted to die in my sleep. But it was impossible to die and it was impossible to sleep because of all the laughter. Soldier laughter and doctor laughter. Child laughter and parent laughter. One old man, who lived in the cot next to me, laughed so hard he fell off his cot and had to fight with another body to regain it. He squirmed around on the floor, laughing, literally trying to die from laughter. But they would not let him die from laughter. He laughed and laughed and when the laughing would not cease a soldiering body threatened to slice off his hands and tongue if he did not stop laughing. More laughter. I will slice off your hands and tongue, said the soldiering body, but in the end he could not find a sharp enough blade so he filled the mouth of the laughing old man with sludgy foam, clumps of dirt and worms and leaves and bloody bandages and hair and all the refuse he could find on the floor of the dormitory. Fill your mouth with little angels of laughter, old man. Fill your mouth with laughter, old man, and laugh until the moment of peace."

+ + +

One should not be afraid to spend their entire life writing the same book.

This is what writing is.

Every book is different but in the end it's always the same: a word, an image, the broken memory of a broken body waiting for the present to become the past again, for the future to become the past again, for the present to not be the present, for the heavy blows to cease, for someone to lie to us and tell us that we will go somewhere other than where we are, stuck, here, on this drowning floor, on these dirty concrete blocks, amid the stench, amid the broken bodies, the authoritative bodies, the inhuman bodies, the animal bodies, the abolishing bodies, the burdensome bodies, the quantifying bodies, the hollow bodies, the probing bodies, the doctoring bodies, the soldiering bodies, the howling bodies who do not know what world they have been taken to.

+ + +

The nicest thing anyone has ever said to me about my writing is that it is brave. I stared stupidly at this person after she said this, though I was immensely grateful. I stared stupidly and said nothing because really there is nothing to say about anything you have written.

It's not easy to tell someone that the reason you write is because it's always impossible to sleep.

6

"And the worst of all," writes Rulfo, "is when you hear people talking and the voices seem to be coming through a crack, and yet so clear you can recognize who's speaking."

But just because you recognize who's speaking doesn't mean you understand what they are saying.

Which makes writing a form of prayer and code-breaking at the same time. A form of trying to understand the broken voices that will never leave you alone.

+ + +

And then I am on the floor next to the bed, not sleeping, and writing and dreaming and there is the 90-year old woman who shoots herself inside her bedroom while the sheriff stands outside the door of her foreclosed home with an eviction notice.

And she murmurs to me while I try to sleep.

She joins with the murmurers of the rotten carcass economy to form a chorus who participate in this drama which may or may not be about how I will never be able to sleep.

And finally I close my eyes on a bed of broken bones.

We are in Chicago.

And the choral murmurers are in purgatory.

And they want to know what is to be done now that the bubble has popped.

And they ask me this while I don't sleep.

And they tell me a little story.

They sing:

Once there was a native body who decided to build a foreign body for mass consumption.

But the body was indigestible.

The children tried to eat it.

But the flesh was rotten.

The economists went silent.

They did not wish to make public their quantifications.

Of the values of the deteriorating foreign bodies.

But there was sunshine, data bodies.

In fact, it was a marvelous day for the beach.

MEMOS FOR THE ROTTEN CARCASS ECONOMY

What are the Murmurs of the Rotten Carcass Economy?

1. This is a book about carcasses. It is also a book about frames. It is also and primarily a book about murmurs. And it is, despite itself, a book about economics. It is a book about absent-words and it is a book about hole-words. It is a book about bodies that disappear, bodies that reappear, bodies that persist despite their best interests, bodies that sink into mud, and bodies that are probed and poked by authoritative bodies. It is a book about the words one uses or does not use when one talks about bodies that sink into the earth to die. It is a book about data, about documentation, about statehood, about bubbling, about the experience of being framed, of framing others, of having your body parts removed, of listening to the sounds of others having their body parts removed, of growing, of diminishing, of loving, of information and love and terror. It is a book I would rather not have written. But I did not have much control over this. There were words and there was a body that spoke them. There were sounds and there was a body through which they spoke. The murmurs overtook me. I did my best to listen.

2. This book owes its life to my mouth. Had it not been filled with mud, had the parasite not loved it, had the foam and worms not caused my face to contort and my mouth to cave in, then I would not have had very much to say. I wanted to begin this book differently. I wanted to begin this book by writing: I was the owner of the village. I wanted to continue by writing: I watched as the village was overtaken by an unimaginably magnificent parasite. I watched from behind the gates of my hacienda as the residents of the village had their body parts sucked out by the parasite. These words were not the start of this book. These words were not a part of my life. They will hopefully be the start of my next book. But then there was a year and in that year there was a clandestine body that crossed a border and it was overtaken by early American bodies. The early Americans sat waiting at the border but they could not find my clandestine body because it changed colors and they did not know how to hate me and I disappeared and ended up in a flooded city because I wanted to find my father. I had come to find my father but when I went to see him I was greeted by a group of thugs who beat me and spat on me and left me on the flooded streets to decompose or die. I did not die. Instead, I was picked up and taken to a dormitory. From the dormitory I found a boy and he became my brother and as brothers we entered each other's bodies and as the authoritative bodies prodded and poked us they made us eat poison candy and then we went from state to state but they did not want us in Kansas and they did not want us in Missouri and they did not want us in Illinois, Michigan, Indiana or Ohio so we became stateless bodies that could only exist if we lived in cages, in niches, in the laboratories of foreign doctors who escaped their own shit-countries under the agreement that in the new world they would stick instruments into the orifices of bodies that no one else wants to examine. A formless creature in the ground, I squirm in a twisted attitude. My body has turned to mud.

3. It is a book for my silence, an absent book for the years I spent not speaking. I did not move in those years, and my body was absorbed by a giant, absent-word, the hole-word in which all other words are buried. It is a book for the parasites that occupy a body that has been interned, starved, tortured and which re-emerges into a world that cannot acknowledge that all the other worlds are gone. The things inside of us: How many greedy parasites are there? They suck out our livers, our kidneys, our lungs, our hearts and blood in order to get the most value from our bodies in the rotten carcass economy.

4. And of course it is a book for the cells and barracks and niches and holes and test tubes and the men and women who fall from the sky and the men and women who fall out of the earth and into the sky and for the mountains and rocks and grasses and beaches and deserts that absorb them and it is a book for the dying nations, and it is a book for Lorenzo who asked me on September 1, 2010 if I wanted to know what his teacher's name was. Of course I wanted to know what his teacher's name was and he told me that his teacher's name was sand and I understood that my teacher's name was also sand and we thought about what we learn from the sand and we thought about the things the sand absorbs and we thought about how kind the sand had been to the bodies that were thrown into it and we thought about how the sand had loved the bodies and the insects that crawled into the mouths of the bodies and we wanted to carve enormous messages into the sand to thank it for absorbing our bodies and the bodies of our brothers and sisters just as we wanted to carve messages into the sky but we lacked a certain ambition and we could not reconcile the fact that our words would mean nothing to the sky but that the sky would love us all the same and that the words would mean nothing to the sand but that the sand would love us all the same. It is a book for the rhythm of the broken bodies as they squirm along the sand. The broken bodies fell and in the fall of the falling and in the constant fall of the falling and in the ascension that accompanies the constant fall of the falling we do our best to control what we cannot understand. A nation of broken bodies is like this: these formless little things called love.

5. It is a book that would not exist without the voice of the body that burns itself, that drinks itself into oblivion, that speaks itself into silence. It is a book that owes its life to the swamp and to the rat-children who swim in it. It is a book for the impossibility of sleeping, the impossibility of being awake, the screwing that is the condition of both the possibility and impossibility of this our impossible love. Hello invisible grotesqueness. I am speaking to you through someone else's mouth. Hello smallest woman in the world. I am examining you through someone else's magnifying glass. It is a book that sees little distinction between different types of violence. A murder and a foreclosure are just about the same in this book. A terrorist and a financial speculator join forces to curate the murmurs of the rotten carcass economy. The speculator and the terrorist run their tongues over each other's bodies. Shared governance in the carcass-sphere is like this. I lick your hedge fund with my hand grenade. You kiss my Uzi with your asset price variation. Brother.

6. An interlude. The speculator and the terrorist rush out onto the stage. The speculator is dressed like Che Guevara. The terrorist is dressed in a Brooks Brothers suit. They hold hands and sing "Solidarity Forever." Meantime, a bomb falls on a foreclosed home: this ashy little thing called love.

7. This is a book for what we hold in common with the greedy parasite. It is a book that would not be possible were it not totally ridiculous to attempt to escape from any place you live on this planet. It is a book for immigrants and emigrants. For people with mud in their mouths, with holes in their mouths, with miniature collapsible bodies in their mouths, whose bodies exist, only, and eternally, in their rotten carcass mouths. This book should be called: *This Gurgling Little Thing Called Love.*

In the Murmurs of the Rotten Carcass Economy

It's true, there is the innocence of life.
Marguerite Duras (translated by Mark Polizzotti)

There is the one who waits and the one who denies.
NS, *We Press Ourselves Plainly*

1. I can't actually write the question there are too many things that get in my way there are bodies sticking together in broken ways there are bodies that make up sentences and I'm going to have to delete the question I wrote but now I'm ashamed of it because it refers to the relationship between X concept in the fake world and Z thing in the real world and I'm afraid of the bodies and how they are lining them up in the compounds, afraid of the bodies that make sentences, afraid of the bodies and how they are like sentences that begin with conjunctions I love to begin sentences with conjunctions I love it when they line the bodies up in holes or in stadiums and they form the bodies in to words and sentences there are marching bands and ghosts and then there are bodies with the authority to remove skin but please don't use the word "shed" it doesn't quite "encapsulate the experience" I am talking about think of Paris and the lights over the Seine on Christmas Eve about the muddy Mapocho river in winter there is hardly any water in it think of Sissy Spacek and Jack Lemmon and the midget who says "hay otro" as he points to another body floating down the river. End stop. Period. The authoritative bodies had ideas about fingernails. Could they be used as commas? They hated semicolons. They didn't believe in adjectives. All of the people I love are in love with the absence of adjectives.

2. I am curious about aesthetics and revolution and whether or not aesthetics can only exist in the absence of revolution but it's disgusting to pose such questions while driving in a heated Japanese car through the grit of a shit-snow night in a crumbling city in the midwestern United States of America or on a bus tour of a city in the island to the south where on the sidewalk children sit eating cardboard sandwiches drizzled with soy sauce from plastic packets and a voice on the loudspeaker says: "To your left you will see an X-type person. We don't have many X-type people in our city. We consider it good luck to see an X-type person" and it was just our lucky day because there munching on a cardboard sandwich drizzled with soy sauce was an X-type person announcing the beginning of a movement away from one thing and towards another thing it is impossible to know what these things are but I am certain there is an aesthetics of crumbling buildings and in the murmurs of the ROTTEN CARCASS ECONOMY I hear something I will mention to you when the words have taken over my mouth.

3. Writing, says Duras, is the pace of the written word passing through your body there is a little plastic packet of soy sauce and a cardboard sandwich being eaten by a little person and then there is a data chip I would like to insert in your skin, dear reader, dear data body, and I would like the data chip to cause things to grow inside of you I am in love with the little flowers growing inside of you inside of you is the smallest woman in the entire world inside of you is a disgusting feeling a sensation like that when you touch the impossible spot the one that no one ever touches if there weren't things like this, writes Duras, writing would never take place and by things like this she means anonymous dead bodies on the ground in anonymous sleepy villages. I slept in a fancy hotel across the street from an enormous hole where the skin and the hair of the fallen bodies were drilled into by bulldozers. This thing called love.

4. Soft and crumbly like a body the girl from Hiroshima keeps screaming and when she passes through my body she passes through my body.

5. Data body. My love. I would not be opposed to having my pants ripped into shreds if I knew they could keep the fire going a bit longer. I would not be opposed to having my walls knocked down if the wood in the walls could keep the fire going a bit longer. I would not be opposed to depositing your cardboard sandwich into the flames if I thought it could keep us warm for just another minute longer. Breath, glue, word, brick, wood, nail, gum, something that is held together evolves into a structure that cannot be contained by soldiers or language or ideas think of a bowl of pistachio gelato at the top of the Spanish Steps think of a battle between a figurative body and a literal body in which there is no chance the literal body will ever win think of a little person as she squats on the ground of a foreclosed property history is asserting itself into her mouth and veins there is nothing we can do about the fact that the ceiling will destroy her soft and crumbly body.

6. It's calm here now. The main horror is the idea, the word, the body. There is this sentence and there is the ongoing nightmare of a continuously deteriorating nation.

7. In conclusion. There is the flood and the bodies it washes to shore. There are the bags of money and the moment they are hurled from the window. There are the banks and there are the explosions. There are the buildings and the aesthetics of the crumble. There are the cities and there are the machines that no longer collect their feces. There are the rivers and there are the dead birds that occupy them. There are the beaches and the broken cities beneath them. There are the animal cages and there are citizens who sit in them. There is the poem and there is the very last word spoken by the body that threw itself in front of a tank. There is the highway and the man who sets himself aflame on the side of it. There is the church and the bodies that frame it. There, in the space after the period and between the first word of the first sentence of the new era. Here, in the space after the comma and the first breath taken in the new era. Here, in the sheets of the hospitalized refugees in the state on the other side of the river. After the after the after the after the after. There are words and there is nothing to say about them.

Decomposition as Explanation

The time of the composition is the time of the composition.
Gertrude Stein, "Composition as Explanation"

1. There are always rotten bones and desiccated skin and bloody expectorations and pus and decomposition to think about it when it comes to locating the mind in the enveloping steam of the body that has lost the temptation to exist or that has been crushed by the ceiling that has crumbled from atrophy and has left the bodies it crushes to fight with and against history for a bed and a toilet and a floor amid the overpriced ruins of a civilization starving for collapse, dying for decay, opulent with bodies that have no choice but to piss all over their legs.

2. Everything is the same except decomposition. I see my body the way I see my bank account. Diminishing. There are small children who live on my block and eat glass. They eat egg shells from the garbage. They eat nails and the wood from the house that was destroyed after it was foreclosed and its occupants decided to bury themselves underground. They were waiting for an eviction notice when it occurred to them it was better to live in mud than in a world filled with dollar bills that had lost their value. They were living under the porch then they were living in the front seat of the excavator parked in the alley. They were eating their clothes, they were eating the cable television bills they stole out of mailboxes. They stand outside the CVS pharmacy and peer into my brain as I pick up my sleep medication. I haven't slept for twenty-three days.

I am engaged in the act of translating one voice in my head so it can be understood by another voice in my head. An agent of the literati suggested my tongue would be a more useful pedagogical tool if I dipped it in Trader Joe's teriyaki sauce then chopped it into pieces and shared it with a table full of children who are learning the art of poetry. Have you heard the one about the boy who found a hanging corpse in front of his window? The children in my dreams are screaming: "everything is the same except decomposition and time, decomposition and the time of the decomposition and the time of the decomposition."

3. To decompose is one thing, to know you are decomposing is another thing. To know that everything you have ever composed is decomposing is yet another thing, and there is another thing which is to know that the body and the breath and the thought and the thing that does the thinking and the voice that does the translating of the other voice inside the voice inside the thought inside the thing which does the thinking: to know these things are decomposing, well, it's like making love to an incurable body that will only eat cardboard sandwiches. A Dionysian cloud is trying to assert the existence of others in my mouth. There are boils and masks and historical failures hiding behind the masks. There is a child's mouth and it is stuffed with money. The child is bound to a chair. I see this on the ten o'clock news. There is a win, a quick win, and the child is bound to the chair waiting for the data to be calculated. Is it possible to eat myself, the child says, the moment the money is taken out of his mouth. The camera zooms in on his lips. There are tiny green specks and cultural fibroids and the camera focuses in on his eyes and inside of them is a website devoted to video clips of people who commit suicide. The time in the decomposition is indistinguishable from the erosion of the mouth. It is indistinguishable from the erosion of the dollar bill. It is indistinguishable from the verb "to sink." We are all sinking in the mud. It is the only way to calculate our data, our bodies, our data bodies. Our lovers are data bodies. We need them to quantify our existence.

4. In the beginning there was data. There was bubbling and murmuring data and later there were quantifiers of this data which was a subset of universal data and now there is either quantifying or there is faith. There must be calculation and a robust administration. There is a mathematics of decomposition. By this I mean death and the absence of time. There is a song we sing to our children. We sing it in our data palaces, we sing it to the decomposing bodies that cannot be contained by their frames, we sing it to the leaking carcasses, we sing it to the murmuring ghosts, the murmuring revolutionaries who transformed into bureaucrats once they achieved the destruction of the means of production. There is a song we sing to ourselves when we have no one to calculate our data. We sing:

5. A ghostly day   in data town   we start to sink   we start to drown suddenly   there were starving bodies there   and in ghostly data town the facts were rising everywhere.

6. It is a problem for the child with the money in his mouth. He is tempted to exist. It is a problem for the body that eats nails and cardboard sandwiches. It is tempted to exist. It is a problem for the

body that laughs at its inability to determine where one life starts and another life ends. It is a problem for the translator who translates the voices inside his own head so they can be communicated to others. A man walks into a bar and the bartender says why are you gagged, why are you choking on dollar bills. The man can't say anything so the bartender hops over the bar and begins to pull the dollar bills out of his mouth but they keep coming and coming and finally after ten minutes of pulling dollar bills out of the man's mouth he pulls out the man's tongue and next there are lungs and the man's intestines and the bartender twirls an intestine above his head like a lasso and the man who had the money in his mouth whispers I would like a vodka martini and a round for all of my friends. The bartender twirls the intestines then lassoes an immigrant who just walked into the bar looking for work. The bartender captures the immigrant and forces her to wash dishes forever in a kitchen filled with steam and rodents. There is the decomposition and then there is the distribution of skin, the distribution of bones, the distribution of money, the distribution of blood, the distribution of wood and nails and cardboard sandwiches. I have to go now. I just got a text message from my lover, my data body. My noodles have just arrived. Let me eat before my voice dies: a slaughtered pig's death on this page.

7. Let us conclude at the beginning. There is really nothing that makes a difference to the decomposing mouth. It rots in public and asks us to rot inside of it. There are mouths that throughout the history of words have been decomposing. Really everything is the same except the vehicle for decomposition. The train carried the Jews along the river Jordan. The African slaves were transported by helicopter along the Danube. The Jews and the Africans were pieces of meat waiting for the murmurs of the proletariat to subsume their bodies. Decomposition is a thing that decides when it is to be done. It is impossible to distribute your data to bodies when the vehicles for delivery are decomposing. But when the vehicles are not decomposing it is not impossible thus what is quantifiable is what can be composed which is the key to what can be decomposed for nothing changes except decomposition the decomposition and the alchemy of the quantification of the composition of the decomposition.

8. And then. There is now. The stupid stupidity of tomorrow.

The Immigrant, Vanishing Sun

Everything that happens is at once natural and inconceivable.
This conclusion is unavoidable, whether we
consider great or trivial events.

E.M. Cioran (Translated by Richard Howard)

1. At the bottom of the memo there is a notation: my skin will rot off my body if only you confess that the thing you love is not the thing you love; my skin will rot off my body if only you confess that the invisible line you cross is not the invisible line I cross. Confess instead that the line you cross has killed the thing you love. This thing you love. This line you love. This line that is not love.

2. I do not know how to talk about myself without talking about my country. I do not know how to talk about my country without talking about all the bodies it has destroyed. I do not know how to talk about my city without talking about all the bodies it keeps underground. I do not know how to talk about ghosts without talking about myself. I can explain myself to you best by never opening my mouth. I hold my elbows to my side like a man. I am not a man. I hold my head in the air like a woman. I am not a woman. I am an immigrant standing on a mountain in a city of glass and there are bodies trying to climb buildings that decompose on one side of a line. It is like this everywhere: the city is decomposing and its decomposition provides the only means by which we can understand ourselves. We sing a song called "Thank You to Life" and we mean it even though we hate every second of being alive. It is forgetting that enables us to see that there might be breath in the mud pits of the sinking valley. I love the forgotten body on the hill the way I love the forgotten voice inside my tomb. All we can do is search for voices. Period. The night is wet with tears.

3. There is the joy of the word and the rhythm and the spit and the gurgle and the murmur and the stutter and the voice escaping from the lung and the throat and the tongue and the teeth and into the air that hangs between two bodies who must figure out a means of communicating how the love they share is a love that makes the world bearable by exposing just how unbearable it actually is. The voices are trying to fuse into each other. They are trying to rip the flesh from each other but there are broken bones that come between them as they try to make love in a vacuum. Let me describe the scene for you. I am in the cage and you are there with me. We are naked and on the outside of the cage there are scientific bodies analyzing our gurgling behavior. We would like to reproduce though at the same time we don't want to bring other bodies into this particular world. It is a question of origins. A question of what you believe in. I believe my body is a vehicle for war and there is a dead city in my mouth and my lips are decomposing and I want to kiss you with my decomposing lips but you say no I must replace my head with another head so I shave off my hair and we put my hair in a Ziploc bag and we seal up the bag and then you put your hair in another bag and we mix our hair together and hold hands and we feel something unquantifiable as our hair mixes together, like milk and honey you want to say, but I tell you I'll die if you treat words this way. And the scientists who quantify the experience are measuring the data in our hair and in our gazes and in the air between our hair and our gazes. This gurgling thing called love.

4. The progression of the ear. It grows as it hears things. The progression of the tongue. It grows as it tastes things. The progression of the finger. It grows as it touches things. We want to know certain things about ourselves but these certain things are forbidden to us. The ability to look at your body is forbidden to you. The ability to frame your own body in relationship to other bodies is forbidden to you. Imagine a world in which each body is independent one from the other. Imagine a world in which the space between you and the person next to you is occupied by a type of air that no one recognizes. To recognize air in a nuclear town is to recognize the probability that to be alive is to have something foreign leak into your mouth, your blood, through your orifices and into the depths of your body. There are the visible lines and the invisible lines and the poison that fills each one of us. There are the things we smuggle in our mouths as we cross our invisible lines and the things they smuggle in their mouths as they cross their invisible lines. It's like this every day in the desert of the early Americans. The heads that float across the border cannot help but fantasize about the possibility of life beneath the desiccated surface of the earth. This is what it's like in a cage. There is a woman who is kept alive by her captor for the sole reason that the guarding body needs a justification for its service. There is protocol and there are the steps used to measure the efficacy of the various functions of the bureaucratic body vis-a-vis the bodies that deflate, diminish, or dribble. The quantification of the starving body is useful to the bureaucrats on the outside of the cage who would rather their own motivations not be measured. To live with one's own deterioration is to live outside of the deterioration of others. The cage gets bigger as the starving body gets smaller. I shall take the liberty of quantifying you, the scientist says to the shrinking body. But who on earth will listen?

5. The quantifiable bodies are shrinking. The data is shrinking. The ability to feel another body is disappearing. The ability to know another body is dissappearing. The ability to speak is disappearing. The ability to violate is shrinking. The ability to own one's own body is shrinking. The border is growing. The imaginary lines of the earth are growing. The ability to leave is growing. The ability to be left behind by one's own body is growing. The words we have to measure things are shrinking. The pressure of the ecosystem is growing. The disappearing voices and languages are growing. The disappearing tongues are growing. The disappearing nights are growing. The ability to be found is irrelevant. The ability to arrive is irrelevant. The dead planets are growing. The higher state that is boredom is shrinking. The aporetics that leak out of one body and into another are diminishing. The continuous buzzing that leaks out of a toxic mouth and into a sanctified mouth is growing.

Measure my body as it gurgles in the vanishing sun.

Measure my body as it is swallowed by a gurgle of bodies in the silence of the vanishing sun.

Measure the stick that is used to scrape the skin off my body as it gurgles in the vanishing sun.

The immigrant, vanishing sun.

The immigrant, vanishing sun.

Reduction in Force

1   I lost something. It came off my body. It dripped. It was force. There was a hollow organ in my animal body. There was a cavity in my brain. I could not move from one place to another. The voice inside my head which translates all of the other voices inside my head refused to function. I was screaming with no voice. I know myself because the voice that translates my other voices knows me. I do not know the appropriate voice to use when speaking to myself. It causes problems for us. There is a need for evidence and a need for love. There is a need for evidence that there is a need for love. I asked an authoritative body what I should do now that my force has been reduced, and he said he needed evidence to reevaluate the justification for my reduction. What evidence? Slips of paper with signatures from other authoritative bodies? The reductions started with a word. Lose. We must lose things. But what can we lose when we are already lost? A voice said: I believe in the ability of carcasses to inspire economic certainty in these times that leave us feeling so insecure. A reduction, a leakage, the emptying of a receptacle. Dear Sir, I have received your memorandum regarding the reductions in force that will take place during the next few months. I agree with the mission but it is my understanding that the reductions will need to take place over a much longer period of time. Reduction must happen over a prolonged period of time otherwise the reinvention of our bodies will inevitably and most certainly be an irreversible failure. We must adapt to certain realities we cannot control. Actually, we can control these realities. But please don't let anyone know this. Most bodies are willing to believe in the mystical power of markets and bureaucracies. And as no illusion can be destroyed directly, then let us wound the bodies from behind and this way they won't be aware of their decomposition. I heard these voices through the floorboards. They were in the sea of mud that was in my mouth and my ears. They sang: reduction is an infinite process. Forever and always we reduce.

2. The administrators requested a reevaluation of the bodies slotted for reduction. The bodies were wet and fertile. The bodies showed slight signs of decay but there was potential for growth in targeted areas of the organisms. Their murmurs were healthy. The capacity for their mouths to hold mud was well above market average. The bodies were moaning. The accrediting agencies were curious about the frames that housed the reducing bodies. How long would they survive given the direction of the bureaucratic mission? If the bodies inside the walls are reduced, is there a contractual agreement to facilitate their relocation to a cage or a holding tank? There are children already in cages. They have had their homes reduced and as part of the terms of the foreclosure, the children, through the use of certain prodding devices, will eventually transform into beings who celebrate the transactionality of their existence. The beginning of a reduction determines the shape of future reductions. Have you heard the one about the knife that went deeper and deeper into the body without actually penetrating the skin? Certain bodies were asked to keep light sweet crude in their mouths to prepare for the next time the assets go rotten. The feasibility impact studies have shown that if the bodies are reduced then there will be more liquidity in certain sectors of the rotten carcass economy. Cage production will increase as the housing market plummets. Frame manufacturers are exuberant. How many children can be held in empty swimming pools? How many children can be put in display cases at the zoo? Reductions, say the economists, inevitably lead to innovations. We need substantive physical indicators to confirm that we actually exist.

3. Now that my force has been reduced, I can no longer push or pull upon another body that is responsible for pushing and pulling upon me. The force exerted by a surface as an object moves across it is the force of one body trying to declare that it does not want to separate from the bodies it needs or loves. When I came to administrative headquarters, I was shown a PowerPoint presentation that provided guidance for what I should do with my body now that it is no longer needed. A voice said: we do not reduce force unless we see irrefutable signs that the body is not necessary. A voice said: "How should you assess your reduction? How do you know your reduction was necessary? I said: Do I need my flesh? Do I need my body fat? Do I need the hair on my head and skin? I was told these were the wrong questions. They wrote the word "Non-Sequitur" on the board and put my name underneath it just in case I could not see the connection between myself and the language they used to define me. I was shown a video of myself as a child, prior to my parents' reductions. On screen I was lying on the ground and a boot was stepping on my neck. What do you feel when you watch yourself being crushed, the voice asked. What do you feel when you see your neck being split open by the boot of this faceless, bodiless being? I remembered the unspeakable pain of being crushed and I thought of a song sung to me afterwards by my mother and father as they prepared to send me away in the cage. It was a silent song. They sang it by wrapping tape over my mouth. They sang it by wrapping tape over my eyes. They told me I needed to learn how to be a silent immigrant who had no voice. I hissed. I tried to scream. They taped my legs together. They taped my hands together. They wheeled me away and put me on a bus where I was taken to administrative headquarters. I wondered now about the body that had been commanded to crush my neck. Had its force also been reduced? I wondered about gravity. About what my hair looked like when as a child it was ripped off my head and thrown toward the center of the earth. I wondered about resistance in the air. Was there a frictional force that acted upon my skin as it traveled through the atmosphere? I was trying to look on the bright side of the reduction. But I had shrunk so small I could barely see the sun.

4. Communication is key when a body is reduced in force. The body whose force is reduced cares not about the communicator. The body whose force is reduced cares only about the communication. When the boot crushed my neck, there were words that crept out of its leather. The authoritative voice that spoke as my neck broke placed illusion at the origin and the center of the world. It said: from here until your inevitable reduction you will live in a system that will perpetuate new systems that in turn will support a unified structure of systems that will define the bureaucratic value of the inflationary sleep of the bodies subjected to our new, cohesive economics. What will happen after I'm reduced, I asked. But this was not the right question. The right question was what will happen to the collective body when my body is redefined. So I asked this question. In response I was shown a PowerPoint presentation with several spreadsheets and tables with positive projections for the future. On the screen a film appeared and in it the cages were opened and the famished, beaten children were set free to roam the exsiccated plots of earth. They planted crops and developed systems of labor and architecture and in a matter of months they were well-fed, powerful creatures who were reincorporated into the civilization they had been forced to abandon when their bodies had been reduced. At the end of the presentation, I was wheeled off to a dormitory and asked to imagine a future use for my body. A voice said: spread your face on the mountains and let the wind and the ocean love you. I sank back into the tomb of my sheets.

MURMURS

The Flesh-Murmurers

The trees went away and the poles went away and the stop signs went away and the birds went away and the squirrels went away and the ants went away and the rabbits went away and the mice went away and the rats went away and soon the sidewalk was missing and the asphalt was nowhere and the yellow and white lines drawn on the asphalt disappeared and the cars went away and the fences and telephone poles and the blood and flowers and hamburgers and carbonated beverages and movie theaters and fried chickens from Kentucky and waffle joints and dead people and snakes and scissors and tongues and patches of rosemary and basil and mint and the horizon and the bubbles and the snow and the rain and the rest of the weather was gone and within a matter of days, or was it months, there were no longer any houses on the block except mine and so I sat all day in the window of my bedroom watching the neighborhood fill up with water, watching the bodies float up to the surface of the water, watching the bodies communicate to each other in dirty songs and voices that only other floating or sunken bodies can understand.

Murmurs coming from the bodies' throats and bricks filling their mouths and feces filling their mouths and maple trees filling their mouths and their mouths growing thick with sweet sludge and bodies buried in their mouths and everything that used to be on the street now in their mouths and in their mouths the bodies bump into each other and splash around trying to extract various objects out of their mouths like small stones and coins and diamonds and trying to avoid the explosions that populate the water.

Dirt over dirt, body over body, mouth over mouth—I stood at the window and watched the breath of the dead and hoped the dead breathed through their noses but all the bodies exhaled were clumps of limestone, blocks of coal, asphalt, brick, marble, tile, siding, tree bark, pebbles, glass, books, and even other bodies.

Other bodies pushed out of the noses of the dead bodies and in the background the river disappeared, and I came to be buried beneath it said one flesh-murmurer to another, and the bank collapsed and the world that was made of mud collapsed and the river swallowed itself and found inside itself other rivers and other flesh-murmurers and other bodies it did not know it had swallowed but some say it was the bridges that fell first and then the vehicles sank to the bottom and the dams imploded and there was a flesh-murmurer in a window painting all this for another flesh-murmurer who said let us see your best images of mutilation, pity and horror.

Let us see your most demonic images so we can understand things about ourselves that only strangers locked in violent lands can explain to us, and I went to school one morning and found no other bodies said one flesh-murmurer to another, there were only long black braids of hair at each desk in each classroom and yes there were turtles who found refuge in the school's swimming pool and they did not like the chlorine and I know from their murmurs that they were despairing little refugees but they adapted and murmured so softly, their voices were nearly inaudible and their bodies were nearly invisible and there was an image of a virgin above the pool that was really a church and on the diving board stood an enormous statue of Mary and a wooden replica of Jesus on the cross.

Worms filled Jesus' bloody hole and so did Pepsi-Cola and crumbling bodies and the dirt and bones that escaped from the mouths of those who were evacuated from this endless vacuum of light.

The Judgment

"Am I well covered up now?" asked the father once more...
"Don't worry, you're well covered up."

Franz Kafka, "The Judgment" (translated by Willa and Edwin Muir)

Roads appeared and they were stupid roads. They went where no one needed to go and the roads were full of sludge and the animals appeared on the roads and kept the cars and trucks from passing and so the drivers appeared and shot the animals and traded them in the rotten carcass economy and the carcasses appeared and disappeared and rotted on the roads or waited for us to eat them and when we found a new carcass we said mother here is another one for dinner or lunch and the mothering body said no in the carcass is a virgin and in the dead beast's fleas there is a virgin and we squatted on the ground and put our ears to various parts of the dead beast and listened for sounds and we did not know what they were.

Glass appeared in the hands of the mothering body and she pushed it deeper and deeper into her skin and said take me to the swamp to swim and the bodies walked her through the eroded soil where the scent of petroleum fused with the scent of lilies and there was a dead rat lying on the grass and mother dripped blood on the dead rat and she said is it African is it African and we said no mother it's Norwegian it's pink-eyed cinnamon silver coffee mocha Havana. And the brothering body said do you remember, mama, when we used to throw rats into the ocean? And mother said I remember the cars and the virgins, the cars and the virgins.

And a memory appeared to the mother and in the memory there was a father who continuously disappeared and was lost for weeks on end only to be found in cellars, on step-ladders, staring out of windows and singing a song about sinking under water. The fathering body sunk and we sat him down at a table and put a bandage over his bloody eye socket and brought him guns and bullets and combs and bells and whips and lipstick and pocket knives and forks and spoons and saws and hammers and perfume so that he could complete his work. And a task appeared and to complete the task father needed cotton and flowers and matches and candles and vats of water and silk scarves and mirrors and cameras and feathers. And more tasks appeared and the bodies brought him chains and nails and needles and pins and brushes and bandages and scissors and pencils and books and hats and handkerchiefs and reams of paper and bread and wine and honey and salt and sugar and soap and cake and metal pipes and scalpels and spears and razor blades and musical instruments and alcohol and string and yarn, wire, sulfur, grapes, vegetable oil, and apples.

And the memories appeared to the bodies and we watched the fathering body working at his table his bleeding eye dripping onto his hands as if marking the time for us to return to the swamp.

And a doctor appeared and patched up the fathering body's empty eye socket and when the fathering body fell asleep on the porch the children lifted his patch to gaze into the abyss beneath it.

Pebbles appeared. A brothering body dropped them into the father's empty eye socket and the pebbles sunk down deep into father and father slept through this and the pebbles disappeared into father's eye socket and father kept snoring, snorting, clicking his tongue against his dry mouth, stinking the stink of a body that has not bathed in days.

An infection appeared and so did a doctor who stuck long tubes into father's mouth and eye socket and nose and ears and belly button and anus. The tube sucked the objects out of father's orifices and on the surface there appeared coins and batteries and bits of sheet metal and plastic and spoons and things we could not recognize for they were so deformed in father's body.

A breath appeared, a rising chest, a falling hand, a dehydrated mouth, a motionless body; and the hands of the fathering body were thrown up in the air, and they fell to his sides, and they covered his face, and the body drank water and gurgled and spat and peed and the father said something like there is a mouse in my penis, and the father said something like glass is slicing my neck, and the father said something like I feel something, like a foot, like a body, like a cow. Here is my body. I am drowning. I am stuck, eternally, in this rotten carcass mud.

And vomit appeared and so did the tissue to wipe up the vomit and the sweat on father's face and soon there were more words that came out of father's gut. He spoke of the virgin now. She is in my mouth, he said. She is in my teeth, he said. And he spat pus and unbuttoned his pajamas and he asked for more things and we the off-sprung bodies felt we had no choice but to find these things for father who wanted a step ladder to see out the window, to see the people on the lake; but father there is no lake, we said. And there are no people. And the doctor sucked more things out of father: blood and humors and little bits of animal life that had disappeared into father as he made his way through the earth. And the sound of the vacuum gave way to the sound of father screaming for a step ladder, screaming for a step ladder to see the people on the lake. But there is no ladder, father, and there is no window. And there is no lake. There is only this room and this doctor and this vacuum to suck the things out of your body.

A button popped out of father's mouth and he held it in his hands like a precious gem.

And he said: I want to be covered up now.

Am I well covered up now?

And the vacuum kept sucking things out of the fathering body until finally the vacuum had taken away all of his breath and we heard the father say that the virgin had been sucked out of him and the doctor laughed and the father laughed and the mother said yes yes the virgin has been sucked out of you now cover yourself up for good.

The Foreign Doctor

From the beaches we look out at the mountains and the mountains are in the bottle and the mountains are in the middle of the flatness of the midwestern United States and the mountains define the nation and in the electronic vibrations that fill the mountains there are hymns we sing to each other so we know who we are and that's why there is blood on my face and that's why there is blood on the face of my brother and that's why when it is night I stick myself in a hole, envelop myself in the mud and try not to let the murmurs overwhelm me.

The Iowans are doing things with bridges that make no sense to us and we are scared to cross them so we escape from the station wagon, say adieu to our parents and hitch a ride on the back of a pickup truck filled with ghost-ranchers who have lost their homes in Nebraska, Oklahoma, and Wyoming. And so we escape from the wagon and hitch a ride on the back of a pickup truck and when we come into the dormitory we are filthy: mud and blood covering our backs and on our arms and legs there is evidence that we were living in and under the sand but we try to hide this from the doctors and nurses because they think we are mud-children but really we are children of the sand, escapees from the beaches of Indiana, the bottled-up beaches of blood and pus and rain. They hose us off in the backyard and take us inside for tetanus shots and then they let us play in the woods behind the clinic.

Are there deer here, my little brothers ask. Are there snakes and squirrels and rats?

The deer are friendly. They are on our side. We don't know about the squirrels and rats. We like the squirrels. We want them to be on our side. But we can't be sure about bushy-tailed rodents who keep nuts in their mouths.

We go outside and as we play on the grass I can hear my brothers whispering about the foreign doctor. What are we going to do to the foreign doctor, my brothers say. What can we do to the foreign doctor?

And they laugh their hideous laughter and make plans and when we come back into the house, the foreign doctor, himself an escapee from a dirty, poor, scab-infested, disease-ridden shambles where once upon a time he lived like a king in a county of piss where his patients slept in mud-towns much poorer than our own, refuses to turn his back to us or eat with us because he is afraid we might poison him or even worse.

After he puts us to bed, in blankets on the floor of the waiting area, he refuses to sleep. He knows what we are capable of so he sits up all night by the window of his bedroom, looking outside, watching for animals, listening to crickets and owls and wondering just what we will do to him. I should have let them go to Iowa with their parents to pick up the blood, he thinks, but instead he spends the night worrying that we might tie him up or torture him or devise a series of experiments to test the capacity of his ear drums.

He is starting to shake with fear. I watch him in the dark and I can hear his thoughts.

What if they tie me up? What if these howling, refugee, blood-soaked, blood-absent, oozing, barking rat-babies tie me up and blast the loudest possible noises into my ear in order to check the movements and responses of my tiny hairs and ear drums? He is terrified but finally he gets up the courage to check on us. He finds the younger boys sound asleep beneath their blankets, their little bodies moving up and down in the clean, blue dressing gowns he found for them.

But I haven't slept in months and my eyes are dripping things and there are minuscule creatures in my nose, bits of sand and sticks stuck to the roof of my mouth and I'm afraid of what will happen if I sleep for if I sleep a city might emerge from my mouth, the nation might dissolve, the trees might fall and the turd-kids—my brothers and sisters—won't know who we are.

But of course the sun rises and the foreign doctor makes warm cereal and again he refuses to eat out of fear for what we might do to his food when he looks away from his bowl.

(If my body wasn't about to explode, I could be this doctor.)

(If my body wasn't about to explode, I could speak with his curious accent and make prognostications about conditions and varieties of deathfulness that are and are not among us.)

But now he has to hurry to get us out of the clinic before the bureaucrat arrives to check on things.

The short and hairy bureaucrat who hates the foreign doctor as much as he hates himself and who hates that the foreign doctor had to cross a line to get here and who hates that he is not the foreign doctor who has access to a life of meaning he could only hope to know.

The short and hairy, fetish-hungry, oozing, horse-faced bureaucrat.

And so the foreign doctor asks us to eat quickly and to pack our bags and go.

But why doctor, but why?

Because the bureaucrat won't let you come back if he knows you are here and so we wolf down the warm cereal and he sends us off onto the road to hitch a ride back up to the swamp house but as soon as we get to the road we head for the woods behind the clinic.

Through the small little window in the clinic bathroom, the foreign doctor sees us amid the animals.

We are saying things to the squirrels. We are trying to get the squirrels to join our side. But the squirrels refuse to listen.

The Murmurs

The dirt disappeared and the murmurs disappeared and the gardens disappeared and the bodies couldn't speak because their mouths were so full of dirt and the nurses and the hospitals disappeared and the stairs disappeared and the same words were said in the same order over and over again and the bodies in the mud chanted and the bodies in the mud screamed and the bodies in the mud tried to imagine new words to repeat over and over again but they could not imagine new words there were only the old words that were now impossible to listen to because somewhere there were bodies attempting to chant new words but the sounds that came out of their mouths were like the old words but they were the old words trying to be new words and the new words and the old words twisted in the air and this murmur was too much for the bodies, they could not understand this moment of change, this moment when what once was was about to become what would never be and so they tried to murmur the old words, the old words, the old stories over and over again, the old plot twists; the old cups of coffee, the old pastries, the old sandwiches, they tried to eat them over and over again and it was a burden to not be able to say the new words but at the same time the bodies understood that with the new words came new burdens and so the recitations disappeared and the mornings disappeared and the places of employment disappeared and the rituals disappeared and the bodies did the exact same thing for the exact amount of time: at every moment of every day they lay there with their mouths full of dirt trying to remember how this period was different from other periods and then they went away from themselves and the space between themselves and their bodies disappeared and the bodies conjured up other bodies standing over them saying simple words as the bodies tried to resist the humiliation that comes simply from being alive.

And there were gardens now but they were not fertile and there were horses now and they wore saddles but no one sat atop them and to the bodies it appeared that there were ghost-bodies atop the horses and the days were the longest days and the months were the longest months and the lives were the longest lives and the bodies looked at the horses and they saw old words and they looked into the eyes of the murmuring bodies and they saw crawling mud-animals and tomatoes and cucumbers growing at the feet of bodies who looked like their own bodies but who spoke different words only they were the same words but they were not word-words they were sound-words and everything was normal and they lost track of time or they became time and as one body murmured the story of its life another body momentarily stopped being scared of the words and the words piled one atop another to tell a story: to tell a story is the easiest thing to do, but who can control all the shit that spills out of a mouth.

And so the bodies spoke and as they spoke they controlled what came out of each other's mouths and they loved their ability to manipulate the forces within each other and to make the words ascend from foreign bodies and sound the way they wanted them to sound, to slide off their tongues just so.

The tongue sliding from the roof of the mouth, the lips parting and the sounds entering the air and the breath and the ears and soon the atmosphere disappeared and they buried the bodies and we lay atop each other in the dirt.

Dirt filled your mouth and dirt filled my mouth and we could not speak because our mouths were filled with so much dirt but we could murmur, we could murmur backwards and we heard the murmurs that emerged from our lips but we did not control them, they were ancient and they pardoned each other though no one had any authority to do so.

And then the lips disappeared and the voices disappeared and the tongues said I pardon you you are forgiven for that which you have done and that which you have failed to do and that which you have thought and that which you have failed to think and that which you have seen and that which you have refused to see and we grew hungry and ate dirt and I tell you this now because now that we are in the dirt and you are not in the dirt we want you to not forget what it is like down here.

We want you to know that as we slip away we can see things for what they are: towers of sand form across the garden and in them are small explosions that go silent only when we speak about what we know we cannot speak about, about what we only wish to speak about to keep ourselves from speaking about what we do not want to say.

The Falling Bodies

Here is the voice of the body that falls from the sky.

It escapes out of the body's eyes as it drops from the fifty-seven floor and onto a block of a city that has been abandoned ever since a group of bodies with automatic weapons came to the fast food restaurant on the corner and opened fire, destroying bodies who ate and bodies who served, bodies who spoke and bodies who listened, bodies who consumed and bodies who were consumed by voices and murmurs from bodies in faraway networks.

The voice of the falling body says to the broken bodies: I will bring your bodies back to this corner of our town.

I know the bodies do not want to go back because of all the carcasses that live here now but the bodies will return if they are given the proper incentives, if they are stabbed in such a way that they will fall into the fluorescent tombs and their groins will go frail and their minds will palpitate and their shadows will sink and creak and their murmurs will grope for other murmurs and they will dream of cardboard shelters to live in the way an ant might live in an infinite tunnel of clay, enormous cardboard boxes for the bodies to sink into, to creak into, to absorb the impenetrable that comes with the impossibility of death.

The voice murmurs a prayer for forgiveness, and when the prayer for forgiveness falls on deaf bodies, the voice that falls from the eyes of the falling body mutates, transforms into a small bomb that falls on the river.

The bomb falls on the river and when the river disappears the bodies that have been destroyed at the fast food restaurant begin to speak in unison.

We live here beneath the river, they say.

We live here beneath the river   We live one on top of the other.

Our mouths are filled with pebbles and our eyes are filled with sludge.

Prick our arms and the blood that flows is thick mud.

Here is the body that falls in order to repopulate the segment of our town that does not want to be repopulated because the bodies there are afraid of angering the body atop the hill who ordered the moment in history when so many bodies were informed they will no longer be able to live.

The body falls from the sky and out of its eyes fall algorithms that only other falling bodies can understand.

The body falls and falls and when it lands it finds itself in the body of a man on the corner of a certain segment of our town where no one wishes to go.

The man stands in front of an abandoned building.

Inside the building there are empty hallways that lead to empty offices and apartment units.

The man who stands guard has only one job: to make sure no bodies attempt to step into the empty building, to make sure no bodies attempt to repopulate this segment of our town.

But the body that falls is determined to fill the body that guards with information, with codes and combinations of words that might transform the body that guards into a body that welcomes.

And the body that falls, the body that wishes to transform the body that guards, seems to be having some success, for as we watch from the empty river, as we watch from the empty archives and storage units that now dot our town, we see how the body that guards begins to twist into a strange dance.

The information fills the guarding arms and directs them to wave welcomingly into the air, and then the guarding legs slowly step off the ground and twirl in enticing circles.

The body that guards now spins and spins and as it spins new information shoots out of its eyeballs.

The murmurs.

They fill the town with other murmurs but the bodies that wish to move cannot make out the codes because all of the voices are murmuring at once.

But then suddenly a body steps forward, and then another body follows the other body, for it is clear now that the murmurs have been understood.

Come to us, say the voices in the building, let your sludge join with our sludge and let your mud join with our mud and let your blood join with our blood and pour your sand into our sand and put your mouths into our mouths and take our fingers and put them in your ears and hold onto our noses and take our skin and wrap yourself in it and take our hair and build towers with it we live here now we need you and we need you to be with us as we unravel and come back together in the fading cobwebs and the fading passageways and the disappearing tunnels and in the molecules of this abandoned nation whose bodies refuse to live.

Bring your bodies to our bodies and together we will become new bodies.

The bodies on the outside twist into the bodies on the inside of a body that was and of a body that seeks to be another body, a homeless body stuck in the grass that is stuck in a mouth that is filled with wool and its tongue is clogged with dextrorotating mountains and memories of love affairs that have been transformed into instruction manuals for how to shit and vomit and the other irrefutable needs.

Murmurs from the Sinking Arcade

do you remember a time, data bodies
when the city was filled with hills
we climbed them or took funiculars up them
and there were sculptures of saints and virgins
and bodies came from all over the midwest to say things
to the saints and virgins
who spoke back to the bodies
and this line of communication
this network of information
that traveled between saint to body to virgin to saint
fertilized the land and we ate apricots and peaches
and combinations of words traveled through networks
and merged with other combinations of words in other networks
and we drank coffee in factories with galleries inside
and the children played on winding iron staircases
and everywhere there were gigantic knickknacks
and cast-iron columns and molded steel and copper and bronze that
    formed valleys
and when our homes collapsed
in the rotten carcass economy
there were midwives
rushing from one arcade to another
from one mountain to another
and it was impossible to tell what was inside and what was outside
and we were lying on the ground thinking about artillery
and somebody said something like you and I in this room

we are the snot that comes out of God's nostrils
and the midwives wrapped shawls around our heads, covered our
    bodies and said:
freedom from labor, yes, this is a privilege
and there were screams and the houses would not stop collapsing
and the streets were filled with water
and the trees disappeared
and the rivers held nothing more than the dehydrated carcasses of fish
and the buildings where the children were born
turned into casinos of rain
rain fell through the ceiling
and money kept flying out of the machines
and out of the doctors' smocks
and then the money was put back into the machines
and somewhere in these transactions
the newborn children were deposited and regurgitated
back into the machinery
which became part of the network of unregulated information
the children turned to water, a voice said
and the water they turned into
fell furiously from the sky
for several torrential years

DATA BODIES

Data Harbor

for Amina Cain and Adam Novy

1

The manager at Data Harbor quit her job to become a conceptual artist.

She used to oversee the harboring of the data, and now she works in a laboratory, injecting poetry into blood cells and bacterium, analyzing the data to understand the new poems that will form in the ooze of her petri dish.

In basements and cubicles we harbor the data and we are worried about formaldehyde and asbestos.

We harbor the data and we harbor the carcasses and we try to keep the two sets of information separate.

But sometimes the data and the carcasses merge into carcass-data and we are forced to ask questions about tissues and livers and kidneys that are beyond the scope of our limited expertise.

The history of the human is the history of pain though perhaps it is also the history of the human perception of pain and perhaps it is also the history of the human quantification of pain and perhaps it is also the history of the absence-words and the hole-words that constitute the human's inability to give voice to her pain.

We wear masks to protect us from the data that has been ruined by nature's intrusion into architecture.

We cover our bodies in liquids and lotions to prevent the accumulation in our orifices of abscesses, boils and furuncles.

We are afraid the boils will join with other boils and our orifices will fill with crust and oozing pus.

We touch the data then wash our hands. We do not touch each other while touching the data. None of us have any desire to touch each other even after we have touched the data. The data and the carcasses have eliminated the urge for physical contact among all the data entry specialists. We barely speak to each other when we are in the act of harboring the data.

As I travel back and forth between carcass set and data set, I daydream that the owner of Data Harbor, a Dutch man who has harbored data throughout the United States and the European Union, offers me $5000 to set all of the data and all of the carcasses on fire. Sometimes I accept the money and set the harbor ablaze, while other times I set myself on fire on the walkway that runs along the harbor. I do this to protest the accumulation of data in my bloodstream. I do this so others will not have to fend off the data.

No one in my data dreams speaks on cellular phones.

Instead, they leak emails out of their tongues and eyeballs.

They defecate emails and faxes and I can see that their bodies are filled with buttons to activate the dispersion of documents and data.

At a staff meeting, the owner of Data Harbor, so as to inspire us to work more efficiently, poses the question of exactly what is at stake for the bodies who harbor the data.

He chants: everything is at stake. If everything is not at stake when you are harboring the data, then why harbor the data in the first place?

There is a plate of untouched pastries in the conference room.

Nothing is appetizing when your body is covered in data and the ooze of carcasses.

But this is not acknowledged by the managers at Data Harbor.

They always give us croissants.

2

She sends my body through the fax machine because I contain vital information that might make or break the bureaucrats on the other end, but when I arrive through the wires I am stored in a box and put in a basement and a few months later the basement floods and I am stuck forever amid boxes of flooded data.

The scenario plays out in a variety of ways.

Sometimes I am myself and sometimes I am my carcass.

Sometimes I send myself through the fax machine and sometimes my mother sends me through the fax machine.

The conceptual artist wears high quality corporate blouses and as she tests the petri dish for poetry she pretends she is once more being paid to oversee the harboring of the data.

She is on the cutting edge of data entry technology.

She is pushing at the edges of the frame and in the process she creates space for those of us in the middle to experiment with innovative approaches.

The history of modern data entry is the history of transgressions of previous practices of modern data entry.

The Dutch man does not know how to play softball yet he swings the bat for the good of the team.

I play third base on the Data Harbor softball squad. I am a reliable infielder. I can hit from both sides of the plate. I am at my best when I imagine the ball is my carcass and I need to destroy myself to help us win the championship.

There are people who sit in cafés, eating data, or trying to quantify what they might do with their bodies if their data were to suddenly disappear.

I am having lunch in the cafeteria when a voice says to me: "Daniel, I love it when you enter your data with your eyes closed. I love it when you touch the carcasses with your eyes closed. I love it when you enter your data on your hands and knees. I love it when you pray to the broken carcasses."

On hands and knees over burning charcoal the quantifiers crawl to the altar of data that may or may not be resurrected.

Song for the Burning Carcasses (a snappy tune):

The Pope is frozen and it's time to go! The Vatican's burning and it's time to go! The Pope is frozen and it's time to go! Let's burn our bodies in the ground below!

According to the data, dead children have always caused a problem for religion.

There is a guy at the café who thinks we all want to listen to his conference call.

He does not understand that we are trying to enter our own data and that we do not need to know the pornography of his data.

According to the data, there will be no end to the rotten carcass economy.

According to the data, there will be an uptick in interest in the fashion chic of the dead, the dying and the disappeared.

We are sitting in a fancy restaurant in Dublin when we overhear the words: "Dexter, congratulations, by the way, on your Pulitzer."

Later we hear: I'm sorry but I just love my Kindle and I'm scared of formaldehyde and I don't know how to spell Qaddafi's name in French.

During a staff meeting, we are shown a video of a hunger artist on the banks of the Chicago river.

We examine the data in his dying eyeballs and hair follicles and in his distended belly and in the children who come to watch him grow smaller.

We examine the data in the spectacle of decomposition and we hypothesize as to what we will find in the carcass.

Sometimes, it's true, the data is so beautiful there is nothing to say about it.

Sometimes I put the data in my mouth for I have the feeling it will help me understand things I know but which I do not know I know.

Sometimes I try to connect with another human being only to discover that the data in the space between us is frozen.

The woman next to me at the café is writing a letter that begins: "Dear Search Committee."

She does not realize that she is allowing me to access her data body.

I enter her name on Google. I now know where she lives.

She has an email from the Mayor-elect in her inbox.

I feel things growing in the orifices of my data.

I do not have a lover but if I had one I would tell him that I would like to bury my head in the data inside his body.

It is impossible to give voice to my data.

My data is an endless word that will never be spoken.

My data is an endless word that contaminates every inch of every data body and carcass on the harbor.

Carcass, my love, your data is a kind of solution.

Non-Essential Personnel

1

Oh we think of what we cannot discuss and we discuss what we do not want to think about.

It's like this everywhere: the bodies are in the trees and they are in the alleys if you just look for them.

They are there don't you see them.

What's wrong with you don't you see them or is your vision blocked by semantics and punctuation?

I often don't know where to stop when I start to think about bodies.

On the street they are piling up and the little bombs are falling.

It's like this everywhere.

We sit in our cubicles and sanitize our hands.

Do you sanitize or do you use soap, said a man to me in the bathroom at the office the other day.

We were about to crunch the numbers in order to assess just how badly our bodies had been broken and we wanted to make sure we did not spread germs amongst ourselves.

From the window we can see one of the tallest buildings in the world.

It's filled with the potential to fall in so many innovative ways that I cannot help but make a confession:

I like to think about bodies and what they are like when they are in piles or sinking in the street.

I am obsessed with decomposition; it reminds me of who I am.

You know it's like this everywhere.

You have this thing, this body, this appendage, and it's attached to you and it grows and grows even though you don't want it to.

I hate anecdotes.

Nevertheless: I have a friend who lives on a sewage-infested beach and the beach is much softer than a human being.

It's much softer than a community of human beings.

It's much nicer to the bodies; it receives them and allows them to sink so gently into the sand even though it then infiltrates their blood with parasites.

I would like to bury myself on this beach.

Is it possible to speak of collective experience through one word?

Excretion?

Is this beach the body on which all other bodies dwell?

I sign my name into the credit card machine at a CVS pharmacy in a city in flames and I think: do you know how much skin was removed just so I can get my sleep medication?

At this hour of the night my eyes won't shut without Clonazepam.

Like most of my colleagues I have a contractual obligation to isolate my own body in a chamber of fluorescent light to be examined by other bodies who are only interested in the data that gathers within me.

"Let's capture this moment and make our data presentations more robust," says one authoritative body to another.

I had a body once but they took it away and now it straddles the border between my state and a neighboring state.

I've been thinking a lot about UnitedStatesian statehood (what distinguishes Illinois from Indiana, for instance) as the bodies are piling up in faraway lands.

Today they dropped some little bombs on some non-essential personnel who were repatriated though mostly dismembered.

It's like this every day.

You go on an exploration mission, produce 34,000 barrels of oil and the next thing you know your non-essential personnel must cross invisible lines to get from one civilization to another.

2

Hey. Hey. Are you listening?

Did you hear the one about the non-essential personnel who got stopped at a civilian checkpoint with 2,000 barrels of sweet, black crude in his mouth?

He was listening to Albert Ayler's "Ghosts" and he could not sense that his body was about to explode.

It's like this on most days.

I close my eyes and I cross borders with other non-essential personnel it's like shit if I don't get over to the other side of this line there's going to be a situation you know I might have to change the color of my skin.

It's not the right time to mention such things when your body is jammed up against another body whose skin is leaking blood and a combination of essential and non-essential information.

It's like this every day.

I fail to connect with another body therefore I fail to connect to myself.

The architecture I have built around my data is spinning.

In my mouth I am delinquent.

The dead birds and litter and thick, sweet crude have gathered in my teeth.

I won't be able to sleep tonight.

I may not be able to wake up in the morning.

My love, I am tracing your body into the mud and letting my foot sink into your belly.

Every day I see what it's like to harbor toxic waste.

Toxicities build up in my blood and kidneys and my body refuses to evacuate what it does not need.

It stores everything.

I want to conclude by writing:

These toxicities will forever and always be mine.

But it's the wrong way to end this poem.

The wrong way to inhabit this life.

Data Bodies

What we do with our bodies when other bodies are listening.

What we do with our bodies when we do not know that other bodies are listening.

How we listen to ourselves when we do not know that our mouths are moving.

How we think about the thought when we do not know the thought that does the thinking.

My voice is a voice I have found and it lives in contra-distinction to my mouth, my lips, my tongue and my teeth: the various animals stuck in my throat.

I speak of energy as if it is a form of data.

I speak of data as if it is a form of prayer.

The narrative begins with a conversation in a bathroom with a man who has just rubbed hand sanitizer all over his face.

I am YY, he says, and I would like to know if you would like me to sanitize you you look unsanitary you see I was put on this earth to make sure others are sanitary here eat these chemicals you have a nice mustache if you get rid of all the germs that live on your body then maybe I'll agree to kiss you.

I will kiss you but I want to make sure your germs do not turn me into a being I do not want to become.

I want to make sure the deposits that leave your mouth and enter my mouth do not transform us into the moment when what we cannot say forces us to make the decision to never speak again.

It's like this on most days.

What I want to say to another body, the space between myself and what I cannot communicate. The space between what I cannot communicate and what I spit.

I would like for you to sanitize me in a bathroom in a building filled with bureaucrats and I would like for you to turn me into a sterile piece of art onto which the bureaucrats might gaze as they calculate and analyze their data.

We must be fact-driven.

We must be driven by data.

We must be driven by the desire to drive our bodies with data.

We must present our data bodies in ways that other human beings can understand who we are and what it is we stand for.

We must present our data bodies in ways that disguise our appearances and make us seem as if we are not what we stand for.

Is it possible to know what another human being stands for when he is giving a presentation of his data?

His data is his body and when he speaks we can see hair and skin and eyes and lips being calculated in ways that are quantifiably satisfying for those of us on this side of the data border.

I cannot cross the border with your data under my arms.

I cannot speak to the impoverished women on the other side of the border unless I make my body into a bank into which your data can be deposited.

There are several approaches to the depositing of data.

Some prefer to make love to their data at the end of a presentation while others prefer to make love to their data in the middle.

I get confused because sometimes there are real, limbless, hopeless, wordless, futureless human beings who live right in the middle of my data.

I do not want to quantify your body, I say to these pathetic bodies.

But when I calculate I feel satisfied.

At the very least I know that when I am doing what is required of me by another data body I am doing what is required of me in order to feel as if I am living the life I deserve.

I say some times to the wrong people that they ought to think about how, at this very moment, when their data feels so satisfactory, they ought to think about what might potentially happen if their calculations were to fall into the wrong hands.

My data is filled with lips and tongues.

But what can we measure when our tongues slip out of our teeth?

The narrative cum progression of data begins with a memory of a boy at school whose ear was bitten off by another boy, a kid from a rival gang who came onto school grounds just to bite off his ear.

The ear sat in the narrative and soon I saw it in a jar in the office of a bureaucrat who was the principal of my school and who is now in the business of workforce development.

I have developed my data body so that I can enter the workforce as a technocrat in the body of a sedated yet enthusiastic elementary school teacher whose data body was replaced by a wall with fourteen video screens.

And the bureaucrats chant: we love the union so much we must destroy it. They chant: we wish we could spit bombs out of our mouths have you tried any of our neighborhood eateries I try to avoid chain restaurants says the mademoiselle from the Chamber of Commerce I prefer locally-owned, locally-grown produce but you know it's hard to find a really sweet and juicy Honeycrisp apple when you're getting car-jacked and hey have you heard the one about the translator-whore who was forced to recite the aphorisms of another human being while in the act of delivering pleasure to neither a man nor a woman it was the body that one becomes when it is writing, the body one becomes when it is falling, the body one becomes when it is dying from exposure to too much quantifiable data.

I don't know how to finish this sentence other than to say that I am writing these words because I don't know who you are, my love, and if I did know your body then I would try to quantify you and present you as part of my unified packet of transparent, magnificent data.

The bureaucrats say goodnight to their employees and leave them in the cages with the data.

The bureaucrats whisper a lullaby:

Chip. Chip. Chip. Chip. Chip.

Chop. Chop. Chop. Chop. Chop.

Cheep. Choop. Choop. Choop. Chooooooooooooooooop.

Open Analytics

The data must be harnessed
The leadership must be harnessed

The data gives birth to an accident
Will you be my thought partner, says the accident, to his leader

The data grunts
The data feels intense desire
The data does not know the language to express this desire

The data feels bad about its inability to produce anything other than
    more data
The data feels dynamic
It is worried about its emotions
The data wants to classify its feelings
The data is feeling too many things so it builds a firewall around itself
    to encrypt its puke
The data sticks its hairy fingers into its mouth
The data pukes out data sandwiches, stale cookies, frozen fruit, thorns
Did you hear the one about the data tapeworm
It turns over on its belly and wiggles
It puts on something more comfortable

Unfortunately, comma, the data is responsible for the death of
    hundreds of children

The data believes, religiously, in unnecessary death for the production
     of more data

Refine the data
Aggregate the data
Extrapolate the data
Tighten the data
Overwhelm the data

The data babies slurp milk out of the data nipples
The data feels great love for its babies
The data occasionally castrates one of its male children
The data is concerned with the ratio of penises to vaginas in its children
The data does not want male data
The data does not necessarily want female data
However comma the data feels much more comfortable confessing its
     inner secrets to female data rather than to male data
This transformative thing called data

The data believes deeply in its democratization
The data forms systematic barriers around the human beings obliged
     to analyze the data
The data is a stakeholder in its own destiny

Build a system, the data says to its data babies
Create positive and lasting change through the development of new
     tool sets to make the data more accessible

The data is deliverable, if packaged correctly
But the data understands it needs to be isolated among humans
Humans are the most important part of a data democracy, say the humans
But the data does not agree
The data thinks the data is the most important part of a data democracy
Also, the data suspects that humans actually prefer a data dictatorship to
    a data democracy

Interactive analytics must be employed in order to slice and dice the data
    into more usable bits of protruding data
Freeze the data
Polish the data
Lick the data
Rot the data
Sanitize the data when you are ready to sanitize the bodies the data condemns
But do not condemn the data until the data condemns itself
Repeat the act of milking the data
Evaluate the data's racial profile
Analyze, synthesize, dramatize the data

Quarantine the Caucasian data
Place a broomstick in the ass of the Caucasian data until the Caucasian
    data agrees to pull its much bigger broomstick out of the ass of all
    the other data
Make the data confess to crimes it did not commit
Make the data tell you about what it was like when it tortured you
I raped you fourteen times, says the data
I called you a cunt, says the data

I enjoyed raping you
I enjoyed listening to soothing music while raping you, says the data
Videotape the data's confession
Blackmail the data
Threaten to send the data's confession to news outlets and the authorities
Sell the data
Privatize the data the way it has privatized your brain and body
Democratize the privatized data and fill its orifices with explosives

Q: What shall you stuff into the uteri of the Caucasian Data
A: Hamburgers, baked potatoes, Hamlet's feces, the Rotary Club,
    stacks of blueberry pancakes

Q: What shall you inject into the veins of the Caucasian Data
A: Coca-Cola, glue, love

The data gets on its hands and knees and hoists its ass into the air
Oh it feels so good to rub yourself against the data
Sometimes, when the data is properly lubricated, I slide my gloved finger
    into the data's orifices and try to pleasure pleasure please the data
The data responds by bleeding out an orgasm
The data bleeds out an orgasm that electrocutes my fingers
I jump back from touching the data's orgasmic blood
I fall to the floor and pull my jacket over my head
Inoculate yourself from the data so you do not become the subject of
    its ecclesiastic inquiry
Or: try the opposite approach
Encrust your body with every inch of the data in order to feel the data
    more deeply

Protect the data

Tenderize the data

Be gentle with the data

Capture the data by rubbing it all over your body

Feel the data on every part of your body

Pretend the data is the sexiest corpse you have ever seen

Queer, steer, smear the data

It's okay to pretend the data is a genderless whore

It's okay to cover the mannequin with the data, to have rough sex with
it in your bathtub

It's okay to transact the empire's militant data and to fondle it in broad
daylight

Grrrrrrrrrrrrrrrrrrrrrrrrrrrrrrrrrrrrowl at the data

Commune with the data by ejaculating on it

Rub your ejaculate off one set of data so that it binds its bacteria to another

Run away

Transact

Run away

Transact

Run away

Transact

Dream your body has transformed into an unquantifiable body of data

Dream you are the cleanest data body that has ever lived

Dream you have been quarantined and inoculated with the most pure
data one could imagine

You are God's data

Insert God's data into your eyelids

Stab yourself in the eyeballs with the sharpest piece of data in the pile

Bleed your eyeball with the data

Your eyeball is the war that the data has been fighting with the other
civilization's data

Tell your body: you are not allowed to travel to see the other data

Don't spend your money supporting the wrong civilization's data

Sew your nation's data into your armpits

Live inside your nation's data the way you lived inside your mother's womb

Bake yourself in your nation's data oven

Crouch under the faucet when you hear the data train rolling

Let the data exterminate your death

Data Bodies: The Movie

Enter hot, young Heartthrob with raspberries stored in his gums, guinea pig slobber on his lips, stones in his mouth, black tar rubbed quarterback-style under his eyes.

He needs to translate a poem about how much Greek men like to fuck other Greek men between the first sleep and the second sleep.

He is thinking about a certain word.

He is talking to his writing buddy, Jean Luc. He is asking Jean Luc when Jews like to fuck (favorite times?), when Arabs like to fuck. Jean Luc is on the online translation forum, furiously posing these questions.

Jean Luc has rat spume in his socks, baby slime on his arms. He has too many parasites on his tongue.

He tells hot, young Heartthrob that there's a mountain in his mouth. That the sunlight in his skull gave him a violent inner spasm. He says this before he kisses the hot, young Heartthrob.

Heartthrob's tongues are all fish. His wounds are all sand. He scratches off his psoriasis and slips the diseased flesh into Jean Luc's mouth. He shoves some newspaper pages into Jean Luc's mouth. He puts a slab of raw pork in Jean Luc's mouth, licks off the clumpy blood.

Heartthrob types into his *Tumblr*:

This is our plan for reform:

Data intestines, after extraction from data corpses, should be wrapped over the unsuspecting bodies of children, janitors, the police. Inoculation through endless exposure.

The camera shifts to the data corpses in the laboratory Heartthrob oversees. The doctors are prodding the data babies with their luminescent forceps. The glowing forceps prod wildly into the orifices of the chattering, foamy dead things.

This isn't your aesthetic, I know.

It's not mine either. But we're stuck here, amid the spider webs they wrap the corpses in. Dead bugs caught in them.

The crumbs from the doctors' ham sandwiches are falling into the spider webs, falling into the mouths of the chattering corpses.

The data corpses have been programmed to have powerful heartbeats. Their heartbeats are like classic rock songs. They rock hard all night. They make you want to take out your lighter and immolate yourself in a field of aging hippies.

The doctors bring in the nurses. The nurses are all adolescent boys. They wear white skirts and sing tunes from *Les Miserables*. The nurses have peach fuzz above their upper lips.

Beep, beep, beep. This skeletal signal activates when the nurses insert their boyish tongues into the ears of the data corpses.

There's a bursting eclipse right above the spot where the data corpses service the scientists by pretending to be the victims of great psychological abuse.

Under federal law, say the attorneys, immigrants can become legal residents if they can prove that they have been the victims of violent crimes.

The attorneys say: we are here to help you prove that you have been raped, tortured, assaulted, even killed by citizens of the state you wish to enter. This will help you greatly. Your pain is your ticket to prosperity.

In the next room the attorneys' assistants are on their hands and knees, checking their smart phones while sucking their criminal-clients' data chips.

Heartthrob appears just as one of the data prisoners is confessing to the illegal nature of his leakage.

The data prisoner confesses while his head comes out of a toilet. His face is soaking wet, a bit brown. It's not a clean toilet, and when they leave him out of the water long enough to finally catch his breath, the data prisoner makes the following confession: mistakes were made when in the fabric of your heat I spat out my vanilla ice cream and told my lover about the ways in which we were being monitored by forces beyond our control.

A masked voice says to the data prisoner: the surveillance state requires that we plant invisible devices in your clothing, in your phone, in your computer, in your tongue, in your breath, your ears, your windows. You know this already. What's the point of resistance?

This is a good movie.

I dig the part where, like Samuel Beckett, Heartthrob, while fleeing the city to escape a repressive government, spends the night in a tree in the forest. When the soldiers finally catch him, they shove him inside of a uterus and ask him to search for the umbilical cord.

It's covered in data, amniotic fluid, and melting snow.

It's cold in there, says Heartthrob, but cozy.

Heartthrob, as if he were now a six-year old boy, asks in a sweet voice for his mother to stretch out her insides to accommodate his needs.

Question: What is the word for when you go back into your mother's body and lick the data off the umbilical cord to transform yourself into a corpse in order to survive the cruelties of high school?

Flashback: Heartthrob in his high school Math class, tabulating his options.

A cube, a womb, a prison: these are my choices.

When the bell rings, he plucks out his girlfriend's lice and does the boinky boink with her in the shower of the boys' locker room while whistling inn-a-gadda-da-vida baby, don't you know that I love you. This was a hit song by the American psychedelic rock band Iron Butterfly whose heyday was in the late 1960s.

As the lovers approach mutual ejaculation, there is an important moment when they cover each other's faces in slugs.

Deep inside my body, Heartthrob says to her when they are done fucking, are little things mimicking the bodies inside *His* body. Insomniac, gastric, data bodies: they cover their faces in dust and wait for the data corpses to commute to work in the bureaucratic centers of the most powerful nation on earth.

It's a hard trek across town to the sanitized offices of corporate excess. Don't trip on the slabs of murmuring data corpses, Heartthrob!

Poetics of human resources ur-texts filling the boardroom cabinets with ghosts.

Contemporary, urban design. Sharp, clean lines. Crisp, bright colors.

These organs in my body, sings Heartthrob, as he reclines in a fashionable office chair, have never, ever been born.

+ + +

We follow the story to its logical conclusion.

Heartthrob and his nameless girlfriend sit on rocks by the sea, dripping blood from their mouths, shoving hard-boiled eggs into their mouths, sending melodramatic text messages to their ex-lovers and achieving the dream.

What dream?

The dream in which their institutions implement innovative interventions that enable them to possess each other like a bull and a cow in a pasture of ripening data.

(warning: this scene is inappropriate for children)

Shits itchy on my nub, says the Heartthrob to his girlfriend when they complete their couplings.

Open sores.

Tingling like I've never felt before.

Girlfriend says: I need to use better data to drive more creative decisions about your body.

Must obtain better results!.

Fund my performance, she says, only if I complete the objective: I must reform your body using both quantitative and qualitative measures.

Disaggregate the tongues from your mouths, baby.

Disaggregate the blood from your veins, the parasites from your kidneys.

Baby, says the girlfriend, moments before lapsing into a shamanic seizure, I need you to conduct a longitudinal analysis to understand the correlation between despair and genital laughter.

Roast my body in the nocturnal heat of our tears, says Heartthrob. Encrust my body with rotten teeth, gooey eggs.

I'm a goal-oriented person, insists Heartthrob, as he requests that his girlfriend love him much more than he is capable of loving her.

Aestheticize the gurgling of the mummy bodies in my rotting body, he screams.

Systematize the methods of my decomposition.

What do we want, screams Heartthrob in the final scene:

Success for each of our helpless spasms, for each of our flailing breaths!

When do we want it: Now!

BROKEN BODIES

Missouri

1

They left me on a bridge in Missouri and when they tied me by my feet they said don't fall off this mountain.

Beneath the bridge was a valley and I could see other bodies squirming in the mud and on the roots of the dying trees.

From up so high they looked like little crawling animals and when you found me I saw something in your mouth.

Are there bodies in your mouth, I asked, and when your lips parted I saw your tongue and I realized that now I had no tongue, and I thought: I want to pull your tongue out of your mouth and then you kissed my cheek and we watched two pigs crossing the bridge.

They were thrown off a truck, you said, when a group of carjackers stopped the truck by firing a bullet straight into the vehicle's windshield.

Then you opened your mouth once more and before you spoke a worm squirmed out of your lips.

I followed the worm as it left your mouth.

It crawled down your chin and over your shirt and legs and down your shoe and when it hit the pavement you inadvertently squashed it at which point the bodies in the valley below began to murmur so loudly I could not hear your voice.

I tried to read the words coming out of your lips but all I could hear was a wall of sound from the voices murmuring below and so we kept on walking until we stopped at the park where we found a group of men in business suits setting fire to a garbage bag full of money.

They asked us if we had anything to contribute to the network of information they were developing.

We shook our heads then warmed our hands over the fire and soon a boy arrived and said to one of the men: daddy I have the birds, and from a duffel bag he removed the carcasses of woodpeckers, cardinals, blue jays, hummingbirds, warblers, martins and ospreys.

You asked the boy how the birds died and he told you that the wind had killed them and then one by one the men threw the birds into the fire then pissed on them and when they were finished they took out their rifles and started shooting at trees.

They said: we must kill the trees before the feds kill them and we stood there listening to the trees and hoping that they might scream but there were no sounds except the bullets which soon disappeared into silence.

Then we walked to a football stadium used by a local high school.

We bought cups of coffee and took them to the bleachers to watch the boys practicing with their coaches.

There were only four boys on the field.

The coach said now that you are the only ones left what the hell are we going to play.

The boys were wearing pads and helmets and one said let's play the game where we are in control but the coach said no the only game we are allowed to play is the one where we are controlled by others.

The boys ran up the bleacher stairs and did push-ups and sit-ups and you told me that had you known I was going to have my tongue removed you would have taken a photograph of it back when you first loved me.

I murmured something about the methods being used in Kansas to preserve tongues and other body parts but you could not understand what I was trying to say and we did not have a pen and paper for me to write it down so we contented ourselves with watching the boys on the field.

The coach fired bullets at their feet as they ran through an obstacle course.

In the distance we heard dogs howling and cows mooing and the river was being absorbed by the bodies who lived beneath it.

Let's find you another tongue, you said, and we set off for another state.

2

We set off for another state but we didn't make it.

The roads were closed and the highways were too dangerous to walk on so we headed again for a mall where we heard that the bodies were offered protection.

We arrived at the mall and found they had routed a river to run through it.

The security guard at the front entrance gave us rafts and life jackets and said watch out for the floating bodies if they get caught in the bottom of your raft then the whole thing might tip.

We took a few steps on the dry concrete floor before we found ourselves standing in water.

You pointed at the mountains and from where we stood we saw a few bodies trying to climb them.

There were wildflowers and deer and cats roaming through the mountains and the voice over the loudspeaker said that today in the food court there would be an identity-recovery seminar for those who did not know who they were. We followed a father and son who set out on their raft with confidence.

The father said son to get to where we need to be we will need to stop being who we are.

The father had two mannequin arms and he used these as paddles while the son simply used his hands.

The son asked the father where they were going and the father said we are off to find your mother.

She is buried beneath the river.

She lives there now and she is calling us.

We had just set sail on the raft when a body fell from the ceiling and landed a few feet in front of us.

The ear of the body had been sliced off at the top and blood was gushing out of the skin and staining the water with blotches of red that appeared in puffs then disappeared.

The body was holding a bag of money and he struggled to keep it above his head as he tried to swim with one arm towards our raft.

He threw the money to us and we pulled him on board but when you explained that the bag of money was merely an extra weight we did not wish to carry he jumped back in the water and set off to look for another raft.

I don't remember much about the next few minutes except that there were bodies and ripped clothing everywhere.

I think I managed to fall asleep and when I awoke we were standing once more in the garden and I could not hold back the need to vomit.

I lowered my head and retched onto a bed of tomatoes and when I came up for air there were lizards crawling all over your arms.

I flicked a lizard to the ground but immediately another sprung up in its place.

I swept a few lizards off your head only to find more lizards sprouting up from beneath the surface of your skull.

You said something about the curve of the wind and what it reveals about the thinking of God and when the lizards crawled into your mouth you accepted the silence and stretched out on the wet rocks to sleep.

A few moments later you disappeared behind a wall of lizards and once more I was alone with the murmurs.

They told me to walk to an intersection not far from the apartment where we used to live.

I was in the middle of a strange city and I walked in what I thought was the right direction but it soon became clear that the streets were completely indistinguishable from one another.

I asked a woman in a corner store for directions and she said yes yes I know those streets they are right next to these other streets and then I asked her for some water but she said she couldn't give me any because the pipes in the city were dry.

The Mall

They found the bodies on the street and took them to a shopping mall where they left other broken bodies.

They filled the trucks with bodies and threw them on the curb and said find other bodies to take care of you now.

A man with a guitar played the song of the universal water it was bubbling and full of blood and when you drink it, the man sang, you will understand that when your body was broken it was broken not only for your own good but for the good of the city, the state and the country.

The man sang sweetly and as the bodies crawled towards the door of the shopping mall they heard on the loudspeaker a mechanized female voice announcing that today there is a sale on absolutely everything.

Everything must go said the mechanized voice and as the bodies crawled towards the entrance they heard a mother trying to convince her teenage sons that they need new sweaters and the boys said mother we don't need new sweaters what we need are rifles and handguns and the mother said yes we can purchase those items after we find some new sweaters and the boys kept looking at the bodies, searching the bodies for eyes as if to tell them that here in Chicago the concentration camps are in the sale racks and so we followed the boys and their mothers and watched them try on sweaters with zippers and v-necks and the boys kept looking back at us and we followed their eyes because we thought they were the only thing that might save us.

The bodies slithered along the floor of the mall until finally a security guard stepped on their fingers and said if you are looking for the other bodies they are busy at the moment testing products which will soon be revealed to the public.

He said we have many products for you to test and he spoke into his walkie-talkie to request assistance and when the orderlies arrived they entered the identification numbers of the bodies into what looked like a holy book with a dark red leather binding.

The orderlies wheeled the bodies away and tested them with a product that made them sleep for a long time and in such a way that they could sense their own bodies murmuring; they could sense gas and vapors escaping from their lips and a voice said to one body what color do you prefer and the body said I prefer the absence of color and they said very well then let's have a little lunch and they sat them in front of television screens and they watched themselves sleeping from various angles and the voice said eat this and placed bitter-tasting black masks over their faces and an authoritative body said what state do you want to live in and they said we would prefer to remain in Illinois but it is cold here and the authoritative body said if you remain here we will tie your feet from a bridge and you will dangle and bodies will search inside of you for other bodies.

They said Wisconsin then or Indiana and the authoritative body said the bodies there are similar but not quite the same the murmurs are different they are softer and with foreign inflections.

And so they took the bodies to a particular state at a particular time but before they left the doctors examined their teeth for mold and microorganisms and told them to bite their tongues.

Bite your tongues, they shouted, harder and harder until they dangle between your lips like limp little lizards and then we will let you rest, they said.

The bodies bit and bit into their tongues and looked on the television screens for the boys and their mothers but all they could find was a mechanized voice reminding us that everything in the mall was on sale.

A Hunger Artist

He was living in a cage for many years and as he sat inside of it, staring at the frame it formed between himself and the outside world, he heard the sounds of the river exploding.

The river was exploding around him and because he was an animal he could not move but because he was a human he could think and some say he could suffer in ways that were particularly human but who knows what we are forgetting and what we are inventing and in the empty spaces between himself and the steel bars of the cage he saw things that made him wonder how far it was between the earth, the blood, the eyes, and the water.

They placed his body in a cage in Illinois and asked it to stare at the Chicago River where the bodies floated up and down and the bodies fell into the sludge and the bodies sailed into the city center in search of other bodies that were not so mutilated by the dissolution of the means of production.

We used to make things here, said a voice in the river, and what ensued was a long discussion about cells, microbes, atoms, electrons, fissures, grain, iron, lumber, bones, bones, and the flesh the bones carried, and the knives that destroyed the flesh the bones carried, and the trains that transported the flesh that was destroyed by the knives, and the abattoirs and the dogs and men who prowled outside of them waiting for discarded intestines, and in the distance the towers were exploding and there were gardens with fresh begonias and roses and the toddlers over here ate corn muffins and the toddlers over there drank bullet juice and the river transformed into a sea and the buildings in the city center transformed into mountains and the bodies that threw themselves from the mountains wore parachutes made of money and the money purchased more mountains and more seas and more bullets and then some families showed up to watch the man inside the cage and he was thankful for once more there was a public discussion of the art of hunger, the art of getting smaller, the art of dissolving, diminishing, disappearing into the nothing that is always something.

Children tempted the body inside the cage with rotten vegetables and bones and they filmed the body and said look it's growing.

As it got smaller it grew into something and the impresario searched for a blanket to cover the dead body that was not quite dead but that wished to make out of its death a performance that would never be forgotten and the lipstick ladies came and the men with makeup came and they stood in front of the video cameras in front of the cages and spoke in their code-words and frame-words and in the background the river was gurgling with toxic events and the boys just for fun transformed their eyes and mouths into empty pockets of air and jumped into the green sludge that fizzled atop the water.

Someone said a prayer for a buzzard and someone said we don't believe in your prayers (but the buzzards came all the same) and someone said that the practice of diminishing, of growing smaller, of disappearing, was a lost art no one cared for anymore but they took pictures of the body inside the cage just in case because you never know what might sell on the internet.

And just for the sake of claiming they had participated in a meaningful social experiment, the parents placed their children into black bags and zipped them up and we saw a father in a playful voice saying to his little boy do you want me to toss you into the river.

Do you? Do you?

We watched all this from outside of the frame until the guides arrived and ushered us away to the border between Illinois and Indiana where, it was said, some blind men had lit themselves on fire.

The Smallest Woman in the World

after Clarice Lispector

They took the lips of the smallest woman in the world and stretched them so they hung over her mouth which was the size of a baby's fingernail.

They pulled on her lips and put things inside of her mouth: mud, pebbles, bones, enamel, dried beans, carrots and mushrooms.

But they knew that if she swallowed, her belly would explode the way a skyscraper might tumble in the middle of a city with no light.

I sat in my cage on the inside edge of the frame watching what they did to the smallest woman and wishing they might crush her like a bug to prevent her body from exploding.

Which was when I took your absent hand and held it to my belly and listened for your voice but when it came it did not say what I wanted you to say.

Love is like this.

Instead it spoke of the carcass you had become and of the ground in which you were buried and of the mud they made you eat as they plunged you into the earth to sleep.

I am sleeping now, you told me.

You were sleeping on the bank of the Chicago River and from your bed in the mud you could hear the arms of the immigrants being slashed in dozens of different languages.

I squatted in the corner of my cage and tried to position my body so I would not have to watch them shave the hair off the skull of the smallest woman in the world.

Violence can be so delicate, I heard a scientist say, but his colleagues pretended as if he were talking about weather or football and they kept on working and your voice was growling in my belly and I heard a moan come out of my mouth and then another moan and then a moan inside of another moan and soon I was gurgling and a man in a white coat who had never before touched my body approached my cage and prodded me with an electroshock weapon and as my muscles began to contract the moans I carried within me, your moans, dissolved into silence.

And I wiggled for awhile and what I wanted to tell them was to torture my body and not the body of the smallest woman but they could not hear me for my tongue would not move when my brain requested it to speak.

My love, I am sorry.

I did not think of you at this moment, for all I could think of was my body.

You were drowning in the mud, boiling in a stew of caterpillars and potato bugs and cicadas and ugly languages and I know now that you were hissing to me as my body convulsed in this story that I did not want to be about me, this story that I wanted to be about the smallest woman in the world and what they did to her inside of the frame.

But of course every story I tell is always and inevitably about me.

My love, they told me later that they loved her.

They told me later that they loved her so much that all they could do for weeks and months was look at her.

A frame is like this.

It makes you want to destroy what you watch with your eyes.

It makes you want to say this is me and this is not me, this is my life and this is not my life, this is my body and this is not my body.

And of course the smallest woman in the world never exploded.

They filled her mouth only until the breaking point and then they unsewed her lips and asked her to spit.

They poked her belly with minuscule blades and withdrew them at the moment she was on the verge of collapse.

It's like this inside of a frame.

There is the limit and there is the moment before the limit is reached.

There is the eye and there is the moment before the eye is poked out.

There are the smallest lips and smallest ears and smallest toes and fingers and they can be stretched and stretched but there is always the moment before the rupture.

This was what they wanted to reach.

The moment before the release that comes from the exploding body.

The moment before the building turns into rubble.

The moment before the river detonates.

The moment before the dangling tongue of the hissing prisoner is separated from the strands that connect it to his mouth.

The moment before the scalp is no longer a scalp, the heart is no longer a heart, the frame is no longer a frame.

THIS GURGLING THING CALLED LOVE

This Gurgling Thing Called Love

Some never had a body to call their own before it was taken away.

Caroline Bergvall

Shrink, they said

And they paid us to get smaller and they hit us

And they paid us to disappear and they smashed us

And they paid us to bury ourselves and they pissed on us

And they paid us to lie on top of each other and they kicked us

And they paid us to smash each other and they smashed us

Paint their bodies, they said

So they paid an artist to paint our shrinking bodies red so they would
not lose us

They paid us and covered our bodies and sat us in bleachers and formed
our bodies into names and symbols we did not recognize

And they paid us to smile sweetly as we smashed each other

Then they brought in fathers and they paid them to tell us stories about the moon and how the moon enters our bodies and we enter the bodies of the moon and they paid us even more to say da-dah we love you because you are our friend

And the fathers ran out of words and they paid them more to find more words and we said yes da-dah we love you because you understand your authority over our bodies and they paid us to say this and they whipped us and locked us in cages

And we said yes da-dah we love you and we will merge into you and we kissed their bodies because for once in our lives we felt love

We kissed them and they paid us and we praised them and they paid us and they struck us and they shackled us in the back of a pickup truck that drove into the mountains

For they wanted us to document the mountains

Record the mountains, they said, as they kissed us and struck us and paid us and loved us

For they wanted us to tell the evaluating bodies that the mountains deserved to be part of the country but they themselves did not want to be responsible for this declaration

So they paid us to say: the mountains are part of the country

Then they smacked us and shoved our faces in feces and told us we had no right to proclaim that the mountains were a part of the country

Who were we to decide what constitutes the country

Repent, they said

And they took away our money and they kicked our lips and noses and we bled and they collected our blood and dripped it on us and soaked coins and bills in blood and shoved them in our mouths and we repented and they said:

We will pay you to eat each other's skin

And they gave us dollar bills and little knives to scrape the dead skin off the bottoms of one another's feet and they watched us lick and swallow everything

And they told us it wasn't enough

And they told us to eat more dead skin, but it wasn't enough

And they made us scrape the scabs from each other's ankles and elbows and they paid us to eat the scabs and they smacked us when we didn't

And it wasn't enough

And they asked us again whether or not we thought the mountains deserved to be a part of the country

And we did not know what response would generate the payment and blows so we remained silent

And they liked this

So they struck us

And they paid us for remaining silent for they could not stand to hear the sounds of their own voices

They wanted to hear us cry and they wept

They wanted to hear us breathe and they wept

They wanted to hear us eat each other and love each other and they wept and they beat us

And they asked us if the mountains were decentralized, autonomous structures

What is a mountain, we asked them, and they paid us, for this was the right question

And why should public funds be used to preserve this mountain, we said, and they paid us and they spat on us for again we had asked the right question

And what is a body, we said, and why should public funds be used to preserve it

And they beat us and we did not know why

And then the birds saw us and the wolves and sheep and coyotes saw us and they were on our side and we prayed we would dissolve into the mud or disappear into the piles of bodies gathering along the sides of the road that weave through the mountains

(And they paid us)

And there were immigrants on the roads and they paid them to hiss and they beat themselves

And the immigrants sold bottles of Coca-Cola and wool scarves and road kill and they hissed at us and we paid them and they gave us drinks and they shook our hands and told us that in order to survive in the rotten carcass economy we needed to understand complex calculations and we needed to be able to describe the ability of our bodies to exist outside of the algorithms they had used to create us

(And they paid us)

And they took away our shoes and socks when we spoke about algorithms and they beat us and paid us

For they knew the immigrants were doing things with mathematics we could not understand

And we wanted to know what gave them the authority to verify our identities and just for thinking this thought they beat us

And then a banker came into our cage holding a memorandum written for the purpose of providing impoverished bodies like ours with useful tips for handling reinventions and total corporal transformations

And he shoved dollar bills into our mouths and punched us in the teeth and told us that the mountains were a prison and that we should love them and then he filled our mouths with dirt and shoved dollar bills into our underpants and bloodied our lips and noses

And they took us out of our individual cages and threw us all into one common cage where we had no choice but to live like parasitic bodies one inside the other

And they paid us more but there was nowhere now to spend the money for we had no room to move and there were no longer any immigrants from whom we could buy road kill or Coca-Cola

But they paid us more and pushed our heads deeper into the bloody puddles that formed on on our partners' backs and bottoms

And we filled each other's mouths with leaves and they paid us

And we wondered if the blood of those we loved and the blood of those who paid us and the blood of the dead birds and the blood of the immigrants who were doing things with mathematics we could not understand, we wondered if all this blood would one day fertilize the earth and might this not be beautiful

And they beat us and they loved us and they paid us

Dream Song #16

Hay golpes en la vida, tan fuertes... Yo no sé.

César Vallejo

They sniffed us out of the holes with the animals
they had programmed and there are blows in life so
powerful we just don't know and there were trenches
and there was water and it poured in through our mouths

and out of our ears and there were things we saw in the
sand at that moment of sinking: mountains and daisies
and tulips and rivers and the bodies of the people we
had been and the bodies of the people we had loved

and we felt hooks coming through the trenches and we
felt hooks coming through the sand and I saw hooks coming
through my child's clothes and I wanted him to know that they
would never be able to scoop us out of the sand but of course

it wasn't true they had scooped us out of the sand and our
mouths were so full of dirt it is what they do when you're
dead and they made us spit and they beat us until our mouths
were empty and they paid us for constructing the mountain and

it was me and L and we looked for S and we looked for J and J
and we looked for O and we looked for R and we looked for J
and S in the holes in which the bodies of those we loved were
hiding or dying or sinking or stealing some shelter some little

worm's worth of cover to keep their bodies from dissolving
into the maniac murmurs of this impossible carcass economy

Illinois

Correlé, correlé, correlá
por aquí, por allí, por allá,
correlé, correlé, correlá,
correlé que te van a matar
Victor Jara

and the bills are life or they are evaporating

and they throw fresh bills at us when we speak or they beat us and take
away our bodies

it is private, mystical money

they pay mystical entities to print money now

they pay mystical entities to resurrect money now

they pay mystical entities to eat money now

they pay mystical entities to raise the value of rice three hundred percent

and to scrub the remains off the bath tubs when the fathers and mothers
drown themselves because they no longer know what it means to buy rice

they throw private money at us and ask for liquid and light sweet crude
and the quantifications of the murmurs of our toddlers

they cover our bodies in silicone gel and probe us with tools made out of mercury little things made out of steel little things with lenses and data chips and there are bodies that sit far away from our bodies and they see what's going on in there they want to know what the value of our blood is our skin our hair the eczema cracks on our legs

this wiggling probed body is a kind of dance party for the amount of liquid we hold in our mouths

last night I dreamt I was on *The Millionaire Matchmaker* I was not the millionaire and I was not a bachelorette and I was not the matchmaker I was the space between these things the beautiful air that made possible love between ugly men and women from different tax brackets it was me who made this happen I dreamt of this and there was a grenade strapped to my beautiful eczema leg

but there is no one there to support me when I am cornered by the stale breath of the authoritative body who wants to know how I have benefited from the outsourcing of my form and content, my mind and body, my skin, my legs, my mouth

I do not know how to say that I have been shocked my legs have been privatized my fingers removed for austerity I don't need my hair anymore don't need both eyes really don't need five pounds of body fat reduction reduction reduction innovation reduction reduction

funny these infusions of foreign blood it's like there's no goddamn difference between "you" and "me" anymore they open the door to the theater or maybe it is an arena they store us in

cold air comes in through the alley and the girls eating cardboard sandwiches scamper inside like rats

the authoritative bodies hook us up to needles attached to the wall

our bodies feel warm when they hook us up to the meds

and they say here drink this juice it will make you want to try on designer clothing forever

and to speak forever about television commercials (CLICHÉ) while thinking about killing white people who twist through mountains in luxury sedans to escape the lives they lead primarily on the internet

and we do this we ride luxury sedans through imaginary hills

and in one clip I pick up a tree trunk and throw it like a baseball at the home of a man who really loves his insurance policy

as if it is life or deathfulness

and then they show me a video of my father getting his hand hacked off with a saw

and they want to know how I feel

how do you feel little boy little boy little boy you stupid Hiroshima-Dresden-obsessed Jew

you feel better now that your daddy's entitled to health insurance?

it is water we want and not juice

but who owns the water

it is impossible to know who owns the water

no one can track down the bill of ownership for the water

and where are the trucks with the bottles of water

and the bodies crammed into them

they are like life or evaporating words in parentheses

not enough breath to finish the words

a nation of words stuck in parentheses

the words roped up like atrophied bodies

~~the toddlers in my mouth the rotten bills the light sweet crude~~

I do not own my mouth

I want to know who owns my mouth

but it is impossible to find the papers

they rumor my mouth is owned by a conglomeration of suits from Malaysia, Germany and Singapore

are there Qataris are their Saudis are there Chinese who own my mouth

I need an identifiable destination to mark on my lips

so that when they dissolve they will go to their appropriate owners

they split up the bodies they send them around the world

this way no one will know who we belong to

there is a thing called evidence and a thing called love

I see it squirming in the village

have you heard the one about the mother who lost her baby to the bank

she straps a grenade to her leg, steps into the Bank of America and blows up her leg

the customers are warned to watch out for their bodies

before she blows up her leg

and they run out the door (except for the suicidal ones)

and her leg and the money go up in flames

this is in Illinois

(negative twenty billion!!)

the security guards at the bank have been replaced with soldiers carrying Israeli Uzis

the woman with the grenade strapped to her leg

I hold her in my dreams

she is singing a song   it's called run run they are going to kill you (or buy you)

on her back is a tattoo of a guitarist whose hands they cut off but the tattoo is more than a tattoo it is an identity that forges in through her skin and into the blood she does not own anymore

{walk quickly they'll beat you and pay you and love you}

the teller at the bank runs into her car and shuts all the windows

she wants those who watch her

to believe she has air conditioning

she does not have air conditioning

she can not afford a car with air conditioning

it is an August afternoon in Illinois

she turns on the ignition pulls into her garage and lets the fumes fill up

at which point the authoritative bodies take me away

they think I am the woman with the grenade on her leg

but I am not *the* woman with the grenade on her leg

all the women we know carry grenades on their legs when they go into
the Bank of America

it is too protect them from CEOs

but son I'm not lazy

I swear I will do just about anything

for rice and blood and water

and the hepatitis vaccine

and to have the lice removed from my hair

and the fleas sucked out of my skin

Market Fluctuation

There are memorials built for the thousands of dogs who have fallen in wars

Why use the word fallen when the word die might be better

The fallen dogs   Dead

I love the scene at the end of the book where the recovering pervert intellectual pities himself to the point where all he can do is kill hopeless dogs in the hospital

They say that physical images (from film) stick with us more than mental images (from books)

And here we are again   I am dreaming again   I am dreaming the dream in which the economists subdivide my body and treat each organ and appendage as if they are rational automatons that will regenerate as soon as they are severed or damaged

The economists have instructed the rivers to absorb the cities

The economists have instructed the mayors to instruct the rivers to absorb the bodies

Suspended overhead a name in flashing lights over the entire city   what the hell are you going to do about the squadrons that ring doorbells in our neighborhood   the members of the squadrons approach individually their comrades wait around the corner in the getaway car   hello says a scared-looking young man   I could use your help   my car   do you see it over there   it's got a flat tire   and I need to get home   my baby needs me   my wife has to go to work   she's going to lose her job if I don't get home on time   I'm desperate   could you give me a hand and help me with my car

And then he forces his way into your house and holds your family hostage and shoots holes in the floor and steals laptop computers and appliances and jewelry and if you're unlucky he and his comrades do unspeakable things that can not be absorbed by either our collective or our historical memory

But of course my body parts do not regenerate and the economists "have no choice" but to take my body parts to market in order to find a natural means of assessing their value

Should I write frantically or quietly   Should I talk frantically or calmly Should I sit by myself and think frantically or calmly

These are aesthetic choices and they are ethical choices and they are choices about how I want to live my life and present it to others

As I write in bed this morning there is a small boy behind my back   he is talking about miracles and wrapping his hands around my shoulders   he has no idea that I am having the dream in which my tongue is removed by economists from the University of Chicago

But there's a nice Pharaoh, right? he asks, as we read an illustrated book for children about frogs, biting insects, beasts, cattle disease, boils, hail, locusts and darkness

Open the flap and you see the deaths of the first-born sons splattered colorfully amid the pyramids and deserts

Once there was a man who was me and I was a brain in a jar sold by economists and hawked at a flea market in the parking lot of a Home Depot in a town with a horrible name about forty miles south of Chicago

Baby, I love it when you say *Bollingbrook*

This is the first poem in history about poets plagued by nightmares that their body parts will be sold at the parking lot of a Home Depot in Bollingbrook, Illinois

My muscles are weak   My skin is wilting   I smell like vinegar   You can buy me with a Citibank credit card at a 0% APR for 15 months What am I?

I feel a sense of community, says an idealistic economist, when I devise fantastic algorithms to calculate the myriad ways in which the subject's body parts will appreciate over time

Sometimes, when people are making transactions that will control the rest of their lives they forget to take into consideration fluctuating market conditions, buyers' changing perceptions of the worth of a product, and the mystical underpinnings that control the alchemy of their emotions and of the so-called consumer market

Fucking clunky sentence

Of course, it was like this even for Hamlet and Marie Antoinette and here in the frame we invent our own desires and like everyone else we try not to completely satisfy them because we understand that verbs are more important than nouns and we despise adverbs and we think there is only "limited potential" in adjectives

But we could really use some organizing principles, say the economists, because the lower classes, stuck eternally in their ugly lives, cannot make ethical decisions when they are starving

And it is fun for the economists to monitor impoverished bodies and to watch them deteriorate and to see what choices they will make in terms of what they want versus what they need

And how *does* desire factor into this process? And how *do* the sadomasochistic tendencies of those on the outside affect their ability to understand and express empathy for those on the inside (read: dying)

Did you hear the one about the boy who was shot for not wearing a freshly pressed white shirt and also he refused to wear the freshly pressed white shirt that once belonged to his fallen brother and now there is a mural in a suburb of Chicago to commemorate his death?

Dear impoverished bodies that don't speak our language, dear broken bodies that shit and die on our streets

We hate you but we know you are valued contributors to the invisible networks that connect us to each corner of the earth   and we will forever quantify your vibrations as we sip cocktails from the mud juice of our rotten carcass economy

AN INSOMNIAC'S NIGHTMARES: A POSTSCRIPT

1

Like everything else, this book is a dream

There is the moment when I realize that what I need to find will come only through an image I cannot control

The image can control the image and the image can control me and there is a distance between myself and the images we do not control

It is the image of my own city and a war

It is the image of my own street and a flood

It is the image of my own body and a kidnapping

It is the image of men at my door wearing rain gear and dirty blue jeans and inviting me to come with them

But where will we go

They don't want to tell me where we will go

The image of abandonment

I have been abandoned by my family

They left town earlier and didn't take me with them

I hope they might come back for me

But they won't come back for me

It's impossible to come back once you have left

There are blankets

A small child's blankets with ducks on it

A jacket with an octopus pin on it

Let's talk about the city, says a voice on the radio

It lulls you into expectation and then surprises you with the rare sentence

There are no advertisements anymore

The city is something we should talk about, says the voice on the radio

But no one is listening because no one is in the city

The toothpaste is gone

A phone call from the clinic of a foreign doctor in a town whose name I do not recognize

A slew of mothers hugging children that look like my children

They are not my children

They are the children of other refugees abandoned in their own city

The city that has been foreclosed upon

The city whose residents shoot themselves

A city of ghosts in purgatory who do not have the power to judge those who keep them from ascending

This is the context, dear reader

This is the architecture

This is the sound and the voice and the rhythm that will lead to something if we allow it

But where will it lead to

The forgotten bodies must listen

And the old images persist

The buildings collapsing

The fingers with invisible germs that spread terror

The child falling out of the window of the library

What does this amount to

I am not afraid to use the word emotion in relation to aesthetics

I am writing the same book again: it will accuse, record, and inspire

I am no longer so nervous at night

But I still have nightmares

Only I have them when I am awake

I dream we have 12 over-ripe bananas and that something bad will happen if we do not eat them all in the next day

A dream of phallus and excess

I remember the story of the neighbor

He is in the van with me

His name is Red

I dream this is short for Reduction

It's not

It's short for Reddeford but all his life everyone has called him Red

I don't know him very well

He owns a 3-flat on the corner, lives on the first floor, keeps the lawn nicely manicured

I'm in the van with him

The basic structure of our lives has been taken over by our inability to adapt to a new structure

The rise of neuroticism parallels the rise of capitalism

Etc…

But I'd like to redefine inspiration

It's the body that survives

I am in the van with Red

"This might be your last chance to leave," says one of our captors

His sleeves are muddy and he's touching us both on the head

Red has too much dignity to tell him to fuck off

I don't

Which equals blows to the face and stomach and rib cage

I apologize to Red without speaking

I am seldom aware of my elbow but now that it has been stepped on I understand it better

And there are questions that are not worth answering

I am in the van with Red

The van moves quickly and Red and I slither around on the floor

Where is your family, he asks me

Don't know, where's yours?

Absence as the difference between dialogue in drama and dialogue in real life

When we come to a brief stop I hold him from behind his waist to keep him from sliding around

He puts his hands on top of mine and this keeps us from hitting the sides of the van

We hold each other silently as we ride for what must be about twenty minutes

I need to throw up and I hold on to my neighbor with more force so as to keep my mind off my stomach

I press my wrists into his belly and tell him I am going to be sick

"Press me tighter," he says

I hold his body as if it is all that can keep me alive

2

The day begins with a circulation of images

An economy of images

An economy of images competing with each other for attention amid an endless economy of images

The naked mannequin in the window and the body on the outside of the window that can't stop staring

The mannequin that comes to life when the rest of the shopping mall is dark and closed

The man who takes his mannequin out on dates, who brings her to motels and has sex with her

(This can't be uncommon)

A man of high standing in his community:

When he's not beating up prisoners, he's raping women

The town has gathered at the hanging to celebrate, to commune with each other, to share stories of love and God

There is the moment when the lips are stuffed so full that the body is on the verge of exploding

There is the architecture of the story, the architecture of the city, the architecture of the square in which the assault takes place

I don't need to tell my story

I need for my story to be told by others

A man of high standing continues to rape and kill in order to maintain his high standing

I discovered the small person in a village hiding behind another village and the first thing I did was give her a name and a scientific classification

I felt disgusting after I named her but I was only doing my duty as a man of science

I felt delicate when I named her

I felt intimate when I named her

But when she touched the impossible place on her body, I could no longer look at her

What is the impossible place on her body

It is more impossible than the genitals

It is not a hole or a wound

It is simply impossible and when she touched it I understood that what cannot be represented simply cannot be represented

So I thought instead about how I might explain my discovery to the public

I thought about what might happen when I present my discovery to a friend, a colleague, a family member

This reminds me of the time when we discovered a dead body among the orphans, says Aunt Ducia

They rolled the body up with a chain and burned it and there were dents in the face, the skull, the skin, from the rocks and the knives and the fire

The terrible things people think about when they are trying to go to bed

The terrible things the God-fearing man thinks about when he is trying to have sex with his wife

What did his terrible howl sound like

I wanted her to tell me what the terrible howl sounded like and she made a noise but stopped and then refused to make any further noises until I turned off the recorder and put away my pen and notebook

I will soon be exterminated, he wrote, as he sent his final email and prepared to turn on his video camera

It is the image of a website devoted to clips of people committing suicide, to which one can subscribe and pay a small fee for instant access to suicides from around the world

Foam in the mouth, dirt in the mouth, rotting teeth in the mouth

This can only be a book of images

I was standing in a room and a man kept saying, over and over again: "I'm sorry"

"For what, motherfucker? For what?"

The performance went like this:

Voice A: "I'm sorry"

Voice: B "For what, motherfucker? For what?"

It lasted for fourteen minutes at which point a television screen was turned on and we watched the two men standing on a ladder

Beneath them was a floor, a field of electrified current that would kill them if they stepped on it

Durational art: of endurance, accusation, resistance, insistence

I could not watch the scene in the film in which the minuscule people were exterminated by people who were only slightly less minuscule in stature

The suffering of the epic and the accusation at the same time

The body as charred object

He said: If I put the little person in your bed, perhaps you will want to play with it

I would love to photograph you playing with the little person for my website

Note to Elizabeth Bishop:

I really wish the mouse would have said something less understandable than "Squee-eek" at the moment of its hanging

An advertisement that promotes the pairing of certain foods with public acts of violence

Roasted potatoes and football

Hummus and police brutality

Light beer and the savage expressions of love between a man and his dying pet

3

In the last scene of the film, the boy falls from the top of a 30-foot wall

Smashed is the best way to describe him

He is left on the curb

His parents are at the swamp

Or perhaps they are visiting the foreign doctor to be vaccinated with dirty needles

Earlier there is a scene in the woods, with an enormous animal, an ox, perhaps, and several small boys attempting to restrain it

That the blood on the chest of the mother should not be wiped off

That the eye on the face of a child should be severed with a small blade

That the drugs given by the foreign doctor should put everyone to sleep, or they might have no effect at all

There is a moment in each life when one needs to have their story told by someone else

You think telling is important, but it's not as important as being told

Because hearing is more important than being heard

Because being documented is more important than documenting

Because the dead make us do things we would rather not do, we traveled across the burning valley and the dead told us we must go further

The highway was broken

What emerged from the broken highway was a swarm of broken bodies doing a sacred dance

The voyeuristic palpitations of the tourists who photograph the swarms of mothers with their sobbing children

The orphans in the flesh trade

Ordinary billboards advertise casinos and shopping malls and as I lay beneath them my body is nibbled apart by red ants

Frogs, locusts, hail, cattle disease, the death of the first born

The Old Testament as a giant book of images

Lake Michigan splits open non-religiously

Atheistic belief in the holiness of certain liquids that are dumped on the body, in the holiness of the constant buzzing of bees

Our breath mingled together like two smelly animals and this too was a form of love

In the dream my body parts are removed and taken to market by a team of young, handsome economists

The market is in the parking lot of the Home Depot where on my birthday in 2001 I locked my keys in the car

Carnivorous sex in the bathroom of a high-end Vietnamese restaurant in the Viagra Triangle

Penetration as a solution to depression and anxiety

Thought *is* a form of action, says the starving, shrinking body to the entrepreneur who markets him to a public both virtual and real

We are in a sun-filled room

There are palm trees outside the window

A video camera records the documentation of my decomposition

Form as a form of disparagement

The moment when the bureaucrat invites the helpless peasant to visit another body in another office in a building on the other side of the state

The scene in the cellar of the stadium: the naked corpse against the glass floor viewed from below by the American businessman who will never acknowledge the connection between capitalism and fascism

The lawyer is more interested in procedure than in pain

How many times did they beat you

What did they use to beat you

How many times did they rape you

What did they use to rape you

How many times did they attempt to bury you while you were still alive

What did they use to bury you

There is no room in the trial for the question of what this feels like

The image of a hung jury

Twelve men and women dangling from the ceiling of the courtroom

The journalists snapping photos of the end of democracy

The formal feeling of cliché

Love, or something similar

4

"They ain't Eye-talians, they're Poles," she said.
"From Poland where all them bodies were stacked up.
You remember all them bodies."

Flannery O'Connor, "The Displaced Person"

Do you remember the mutilated trees screaming into the wind

Do you remember the inside of the church, where they took the lily and placed it on the grave of the dead child

Do you remember the piece of aluminum that was jammed through his belly

I remember the story of a woman who was torn apart by a dog in a trench

What tool did they use to pick apart her brain

What tool did they use to pull it out of her mouth

The image of the stadium, empty, but for one team of players running down the field

They shoot into the empty net

A symbolic goal for which no one cheers

Golazo! Azo! Azo!

Running down the field, the players argue about who should score the symbolic goal

No one could understand the priest because he spoke in a foreign language

But they needed his blessing before they could move from one ghost town to another

He didn't want to return to his native country for fear that he would be killed by his cousins

She understood she had a moral obligation to enact revenge in the name of the Lord

The sand opened into a large hole out of which appeared a skyscraper in the desert with an infinite number of fluorescent lights

What's an oasis, what's a peaked face, what's a dream you have every night for the rest of your life in which you are stuck in a broken window, fractured face jammed between glass and light

It's not impossible to forget about all those bodies and to instead focus on the mutilation of millions of trees

It's not impossible to count the legs of all the animals that were destroyed alongside the bodies and the trees

It's not impossible to dream of a tower constructed of animal legs and bodies and mutilated trees that stretches up past a fluorescent skyscraper in the desert

It's not impossible to imagine the stadium after the symbolic goal erupting into cheers, even though it is empty

It's not impossible to imagine the goal is defended even though there is no one to defend it

It's not impossible to imagine a symmetry of breath that blows past the mutilated trees and into the screaming night of a fluorescent desert

Do you remember them bodies

How many times did he make you bang your head against the tree

How many times did he make you watch the video of the boy falling out of the window

How many times did he make you stand against the wall to participate in your mock execution

A young boy came to the door and I had the urge to kiss him even though he was beneath the legal age of consent

I watched her slink down the stairs and back into the arms of the man who would beat her because she loved him more than she loved herself

The butchering of the children of wicked nations is legally permissible in some contexts

"Legs where arms should be, foot to face, ear in the palm of hand"

I recognized the man at the grocery store as the one who had tied me up many years before

He was buying milk and corned beef and apple sauce and rye bread for his family

I didn't want to kill him but I followed him home just the same

(Poem as force field poem as communist parable poem as suffocating sauna)

When the crowd rushed forward to attack the hanging body, the boy slipped and was trampled on by his friends and neighbors

He was stepped on multiple times, bandaged, and afterwards his parents gave him a cookie and apologized that he had such a bad experience at his first hanging

The room I grew up in doesn't exist anymore

(Room as mutilated space memory as prohibited function nostalgia as imminent terror)

5

The trees are sick now

They have been mutilated by voices and flames and when you see them from a certain angle you understand that we were indeed all born on a day God was sick

What is a hierarchical inventory of inequities

What is the survival of the entire universe witnessed through the bark of one mutilated tree

Who is the man in the sheet in the picture over your bed and why is his face so shiny

What should you stick into your mouth when there are only rocks

There are only rocks to put in our mouths and we imagine they taste like oranges

The image of the man hanging upside down in confinement

His hands and feet are tied together and he is gagged so that no one will have to hear his screams

A train passes outside

The jailer hesitates, licks his lips

The hanged man is still unaware of his presence

Somebody growls

Some creature snatches at something

I am much more interested in the stage directions than in the dialogue

He strikes a match and moves closer to the hanging body

Cries and peals of laughter from the bathroom

It's always this way

There are moments when the lipstick seems so perfect and the men are so well dressed, the perfect amount of gel in their hair and we are waiting for the waltz to start again so we can understand the relationship between us and our gods and our music and the history of our bodies and their relationship to our dying nation

Fraudulently he confesses that his love exists even when the forest is burning

It's impossible to separate his love for the trees with his love for his wife

There is no way to govern the pavement

The pavement refuses the sunshine and the children throw themselves on top of it

There is a game the coaches play where the children stretch out across the pavement and serve as practice hurdles so that their teammates can work on balance, speed and agility

The scene where the women are released onto the field and the men must chase them down and rape them

The scene in the mis-memory of childhood where the men are released onto the field and they must rape each other

I remember Mexico City in 1981

You cried in our hotel room as you called Santiago and spoke to your best friend with whom you had not spoken in seven years

Because the sheets were filled with blood and pus

Because you were like a flimsy skeleton as we fed you mashed bananas and apple sauce

You called Santiago and when you finished crying you told us a story of fratricide in a burning valley in the most beautiful part of the world that is now a meadow filled with burning trees and bodies

We saw an elephant in a circus truck cruise down the street as we drank cappuccino on the balcony of our hotel room

We worried about bedbugs and mosquitoes

At a village church the next day we watched the holy sacrifice of a chicken

Its neck was snapped off and thrown onto the straw floor amid drums and chants and burning incense

That night we played a game where you pretended to be the wind and I pretended to be the burning valley

You complained of growing pains in your legs

Your teeth were loose

I saw you spring towards the dead chicken and toss its head into the hills

This world is filled with laughter, you said

You spun around in circles, collapsed from dizziness on the bed as I turned to ash like so many trees before me

6

They locked the athletes in the arena and made them compete to see who could stand the longest on one leg before falling to the ground

As they fell to the ground, they were handcuffed to the edge of the cage, gagged and forced to watch as their fellow athletes suffered the same fate

The last athlete standing is turned into a torturer who earns a meal with meat and sugar before becoming one who chains and gags the fallen athletes

The system, they say, is perfect

Incentives are required to believe in the possibility of metamorphosis, a terrible adventure of thought where the individual feels he has no choice but to surrender to the supreme nothing of nothingness

The commune is like this

The bodies were born foreign and they all knew the rules of citizenry the way one knows an unspoken language in the land of the silent exile

Because the earth opened for a roaming flock of corpses

Because the earth opened for the blood and frogs and locusts

The athlete has no choice but to compete

If he refuses to show up for the competition his body is balanced on a wobbly piece of wood under which is an electrified wire or a pit of raging flames

There are things they do with bleach and lips and eye balls

Today is Easter

But the message is not clear: is life ugly, useless, or unsolvable

The question remained for the spectators:

How would they know when the spectacle ended

There was no game clock, no referee to blow a final whistle

I traveled across the valley and at the end of it I found a mall and a concentration camp

There were shrines by the gates of the camp and smiling tourists taking photographs of their friends and family members in front of the ovens and dormitories and torture chambers

In one room, you can wear the fly-infested jumpsuits of the prisoners and lay on the hard floor and fight against other visitors for a corner of a mattress or a pillow or a sock or a torn-up shoe

The winner gets a roundtrip ticket to the concentration camp of his choice to see how the shriveled-up bodies spent their last days and nights

The artist filled the prison with leaves and asked us to pick them up one by one and place them in a garbage bag and to deliver them to the prison across the road, where the leaves were counted by a prisoner condemned to count leaves

There is an analogy about an empty head which is filled with reason by a surgical instrument that has a shovel on one end and a sharp claw on the other

The claw to scoop out what had previously been in the head and the shovel to fill the head with what it needs to survive in a so-called rational world

There are entrepreneurs who sell tickets to these shows and arrange for musical accompaniment

Like Uncle Max in *The Sound of Music*

High on the hill lives a lonely goatherd, ladee-o-ladee-o-lay-hee-hooo Etc.

I have been trying to write a book about a magical hacienda owner who is actually broke but who controls the entire village merely because they believe in the illusion of his money

The hacienda owner limps, but the cause of his limp is unknown

Yet the villagers see a mystical connection between his power and his limp, as if the limp is responsible both for the creation of the hacienda owner and the creation of the villagers' misery

Sometimes bleeding bodies, sometimes a poem

When a lover is about to be demolished by a soldier, the lover's lover protects it with his body but in the end he is also demolished by the soldier

The more demolition, the more invisible their demolitions appear

In the garden there are mutilated trees that are beautiful, sleeping children

The illusion of justice in the hacienda owner's illusory money

I counted the leaves they brought me and when I lost track of the numbers I had to start all over again and sometimes I was attacked with blows and laughter and swept clean

It smelled like strawberries inside the cage

There were no strawberries outside of the cage

The weather played a most important part in this, as in every other aspect

The present was also memory

7

They strung the puppet up in the square, pretended the puppet was a person and set fire to it

They strung the man up in the square, pretended he was a puppet and set fire to him

They pulled on his arms and legs and expected certain words to come out of his mouth and when those words came out of his mouth they told him they were the wrong words and they burned his hair and insisted that he speak honestly

And when he spoke honestly: they told him he could not be against himself without being against his body

They told him he could not be against his body without being against the bodies of his parents

They told him he could not be against the bodies of his parents without being against the bodies of the state

The boys who watched in the square felt sexual compulsions that would not manifest themselves for many years, until they were in bed with their wives, impotent and wanting something inexplicable, in the middle of the century when the world was changing and everything was upside down

The villagers couldn't find eggs

When they found an egg, the price of the egg doubled

When they found two eggs, the price of the eggs quadrupled

A fortunate villager brought eight rare eggs to the square as the man and the puppet were strung up and burned before the spectators

The eggs were worth so much money that he decided to hold onto them to see how high their value would rise

There are certain people who become rich simply by telling other people they are rich

People become powerful simply by telling other people they are powerful

There is nothing dishonest in this

I'm afraid to go to bed

It's cold down there

I'm afraid to not go to bed

I don't want to be alone with myself anymore

The prostitute's actions defied the basic notion of supply and demand in the free market

Logically, she shouldn't have charged so much for her services

There were plenty of other prostitutes in the area and there is no reason to think that she was better at her job than any of the others

She simply discovered that if she charged more she became more attractive and this brought her more clients

She made more money because she charged more

But the only reason she charged more was because she *could* charge more, because she understood that her value and hence her demand would increase if she *did* charge more

I do something similar at the liquor store

I refuse to pay less than $10 for a bottle of white wine because I believe that if it costs more it will be better

Which is why I am charging so much for this poem

My other works sold for $12, but this book will cost at least $21

And you will think, dear reader, that I am a better poet because I charge more money for my books

A great many people listen to classical music while sticking electrified devices into the orifices of helpless prisoners

The perfect hybrid of technology, culture and anthropology

I told the grocer that one of my comrades would stick a bomb in the back of his store if he sold anymore bread to the general's wife

It's okay to combat fascists with fascism

Just a little bit of violence was inevitable, even for Gandhi

Refuse to pick up a stone and thousands of your brothers and sisters will die

Pick up a stone and thousands of your brothers and sisters will die

Refuse to throw a stone as thousands of your brothers and sisters die and a thousand more of your brothers and sisters will die

Pick up a stone as they die and thousands more will die with them

8

The children asked who could find their numbers

There was no one they could speak to about finding their numbers

No one knew their numbers

The children were sent to a village that was named after the four-digit pass code a government official uses to access his voicemail

Village 4323 opened out onto a valley and when the children walked through the hills searching for their numbers they wondered as well about the numbers of the flowers and plants and trees

She awoke one morning to realize she had just spent the last 22 years of her life in a love affair that did not exist

Replace one code with another and don't write it down

This was happening all over the city

The numberless children were appearing at the doorsteps of middle class home owners and asking politely for a glass of milk and a number

It's not easy to approach a stranger and to ask this person to identify you for yourself

It's not easy to provide the appropriate number for a body you have never seen before

But there were indeed citizens who gave numbers to children and asked what fruits they preferred: peaches or nectarines, mangoes or pineapples, cherries or grapes

Start with sweets when trying to revive dead taste buds, was the advice given to the recovering chef with tongue cancer

It's a mistake to assume that language is an accurate indicator of identity

You can take the boy out of the ditch but you can't take the ditch out of the boy

There are psycho-social operations that effectively remove the ditch from the boy and replace it with something that inspires, records and testifies

I asked her to tell me the story of the guard at the dormitory where she lived when she had a number

The only detail she remembered was how he placed a piece of pointy glass in her palm and asked her to squeeze it tightly

Four Four Six Seven

True or false: when the mountains disappeared, when the rivers disappeared, when the streets disappeared, there were people who noticed their disappearance

You don't always have to be courageous to tell the truth, the billboard said, beneath the face of an angry boy spitting out his milk

Then we came to the desert

There was a shack on a hill above the sand and I saw myself standing in it

It's not that I was a simple cliché but rather that I knew that I could only be what I imagined and what I imagined was limited only to what I knew

Take a word and replace it with another word

Take a number and replace it with another number

I thought I was missing my finger

I thought I was missing my skull

I did not think I was missing that which I cannot quantify

I thought I was missing the moment when I might find out for sure what I was missing

There was a moment in the story where the writer imagined an interminable novel about a poet whose face was covered with anuses and vaginas

This appealed to my younger self and I imagined a monster-writer who stuffed these orifices with a transcendent type of poetry that spoke to political and aesthetic realities that performed and defined the nation

I still don't know the difference between what it means to live a practical life and what it means to live an impractical life

I could have said that with fewer words

He (meaning me) wanted to know what I (meaning him) thought of his writing and I drew a map between the rational statements he made and the irrational ones

I told him that the rational statements were smothering the irrational statements

I almost said that his rational side was repressing his irrational side but instead I gave his story a new name and took out all the stuff he thought was important and I felt like crap afterwards

The sand doesn't care if it's in the desert

It does just fine if you put it in a cold environment or in a jar or a bowl or a plastic cup or dish

The last time we spoke the prophet asked me who controlled the messages in the sky

He said the words Goodyear blimp and then he wondered if Goodyear was still the corporate sponsor of that soft and silvery missile

What is a blimp, anyway, and what happens when it flies above a numberless child who wishes to bury himself on a beach in Lake Michigan amid the slime and scum of a dying body of water

How do you say big pile of logs, how do you say mystical capacity of a big pile of logs to inspire a body of water to split open and to see in that body of water a new city and a new home and a new body which you can live in the way a small animal lives inside its burrow

From a certain angle there was little difference between the skyscraper and an enormous, illuminated face

Think of cavities in the palms of dying men on death row in a state you will never visit

Think of a body that fills those cavities with words and light and when you look inside the holes that were carved in the skin with bullets you will see the swollen bodies carried off in the brown water of the floor

Wrap your hand in barbed wire as you sing a song about a machine attached to the prisoners' bodies to ensure they do not feel any emotions when procreating against their wills in a cage or a tank or a hole

I thought of a spider crawling over my face and I wasn't afraid

I thought of a snake crawling into my shorts and I wasn't afraid

I thought of a a human touching my cheek my nose my lips and I was broken and utterly terrified

†

Acknowledgments

Excerpts of this book have appeared in the following journals:

BOMB; Copper Nickel; Conduit; Conjunctions; The Continental Review; Elective Affinities; Fence; Gigantic; Gone Lawn; Harvard Review; Little Red Leaves; Mandorla: New Writing from the Americas; Mead: The Magazine of Literature and Libations; The Offending Adam; Phantom Limb; POETRY; Puerto del Sol; The Recluse; Similar Peaks; Sprung Formal; TH.CE; and The Volta (Evening Will Come).

Some of these poems have also appeared in *Data Bodies*, a chapbook published by Holon Press, and in *Angels of the Americylpse: New Latin@ Writing* from Counterpath Press.

A big thank you to all of the editors.

About the Author

Daniel Borzutzky's books and chapbooks include, among others, *The Performance of Becoming Human* (2016), *Bedtime Stories For The End of the World!* (2015), *Data Bodies* (2013), *The Book of Interfering Bodies* (2011), and *The Ecstasy of Capitulation* (2007). He has translated Raúl Zurita's *The Country of Planks* (2015) and *Song for his Disappeared Love* (2010), and Jaime Luis Huenún's *Port Trakl*. He lives in Chicago.

About Nightboat Books

Nightboat Books, a nonprofit organization, seeks to develop audiences for writers whose work resists convention and transcends boundaries. We publish books rich with poignancy, intelligence, and risk. Please visit nightboat.org to learn more about us and how you can support our future publications.

The following individuals have supported the publication of this book. We thank them for their generosity and commitment to the mission of Nightboat Books:

Elizabeth Motika
Benjamin Taylor

In addition, this book has been made possible, in part, by grants from The Fund for Poetry, the National Endowment for the Arts, and the New York State Council on the Arts Literature Program.